AF814418

Be a TOP SCORER
in CBSE Exams 2025

i Succeed

10 Sample Question Papers

with Quick Study Notes

Information Technology 10th

Code-402

arihant
SUCCESS AND NOTHING LESS

Be a TOP SCORER
in CBSE Exams 2025

i Succeed

10 Sample Question Papers

with Quick Study Notes

Information Technology 10th

Code-402

AUTHOR
Chhirja Yadav

List of *i Succeed* Sample Papers for CBSE 10

- Mathematics Standard
- Mathematics Basic
- Science
- Social Science
- English Language & Literature
- English Communicative
- Computer Applications
- Artificial Intelligence
- Information Technology
- हिंदी 'अ'
- हिंदी 'ब'
- संस्कृतम्
- सामाजिक विज्ञान
- विज्ञान
- गणित

Arihant Prakashan
(School Division Series)

卐 **Administrative & Production Offices**

Regd. Office

'Ramchhaya' 4577/15, Agarwal Road, Darya Ganj, New Delhi -110002
Tele: 011- 47630600, 43518550

卐 **Head Office**

Kalindi, TP Nagar, Meerut (UP) - 250002
Tel: 0121-7156203, 7156204

卐 **Sales & Support Offices**

Agra, Ahmedabad, Bengaluru, Bareilly, Chennai, Delhi, Guwahati, Hyderabad, Jaipur, Jhansi, Kolkata, Lucknow, Nagpur & Pune.

卐 **PRICE** ₹200.00

PO No : TXT-XX-XXXXXXX-X-XX

Published by Arihant Publications (India) Ltd.

For further information about the books published by Arihant, log on to www.arihantbooks.com or e-mail at info@arihantbooks.com

Follow us on

i Succeed

SAMPLE QUESTION PAPERS

THE **BEST CHOICE** OF TEACHERS & STUDENTS, Why?

01 Exact Exam Pattern

All Sample Papers have been designed on the actual exam format of CBSE

02 Complete Syllabus

Complete coverage of syllabus through different types of questions across all the sample papers

03 50% CBQs

As per latest CBSE circular, each sample paper has 50% Competency based Questions of all types.

04 Detailed Answers

Step-by-step answers to help you understand concepts and improve problem-solving skills.

05 Quick Study Notes

Focused revision of the whole syllabus through Quick Study Notes.

Free Doubt Solving APP

To help you sort out your doubts at any time any place.

i Succeed

Information Technology 10th Code 402

Course Structure
2024-25

<table>
<tr><th></th><th>Units</th><th colspan="2">No. of Hours for Theory and Practical</th><th>Max. Marks for Theory and Practical</th></tr>
<tr><td rowspan="7">PART A</td><td>Employability Skills</td><td colspan="2"></td><td></td></tr>
<tr><td>Unit 1: Communication Skills-II</td><td colspan="2">10</td><td>2</td></tr>
<tr><td>Unit 2: Self-Management Skills-II</td><td colspan="2">10</td><td>3</td></tr>
<tr><td>Unit 3: ICT Skills-II</td><td colspan="2">10</td><td>1</td></tr>
<tr><td>Unit 4: Entrepreneurial Skills-II</td><td colspan="2">15</td><td>3</td></tr>
<tr><td>Unit 5: Green Skills-II</td><td colspan="2">05</td><td>1</td></tr>
<tr><td>Total</td><td colspan="2">50</td><td>10</td></tr>
<tr><td rowspan="6">PART B</td><td>Subject Specific Skills</td><td>Theory</td><td>Practical</td><td>Marks</td></tr>
<tr><td>Unit 1: Digital Documentation (Advanced)</td><td>12</td><td>18</td><td>8</td></tr>
<tr><td>Unit 2: Electronic Spreadsheet (Advanced)</td><td>15</td><td>23</td><td>10</td></tr>
<tr><td>Unit 3: Database Management System</td><td>18</td><td>27</td><td>12</td></tr>
<tr><td>Unit 4: Maintain Health, Safety and Secure Working Environment</td><td>15</td><td>22</td><td>10</td></tr>
<tr><td>Total</td><td>60</td><td>90</td><td>40</td></tr>
<tr><td rowspan="7">PART C</td><td>Practical Work</td><td colspan="2"></td><td>Marks</td></tr>
<tr><td>Practical Examination</td><td colspan="2"></td><td></td></tr>
<tr><td>• Advanced Documentation</td><td colspan="2">5 Marks</td><td rowspan="3">20</td></tr>
<tr><td>• Advanced Spreadsheets</td><td colspan="2">5 Marks</td></tr>
<tr><td>• Databases</td><td colspan="2">10 Marks</td></tr>
<tr><td>• Viva Voce</td><td colspan="2">10 Marks</td><td>10</td></tr>
<tr><td>Total</td><td colspan="2"></td><td>30</td></tr>
</table>

	Project Work/Field Visit		Marks
PART D	Any Interdisciplinary Real World Case Study to be taken. Summarized data reports of same can be presented in base. Input should be taken using forms and output should be done using reports using base. Documentation of the case study should be presented using writer.		10
	PORTFOLIO/ PRACTICAL FILE: (Portfolio should contain printouts of the practical done using Writer, Calc and Base with minimum 5 problems of each)		10
	Total		**20**
	Grand Total	**200**	**100**

BLUE-PRINT

For Sample Question Paper for Class X

Max. Time : 2 Hours
Max. Marks : 50

PART A - EMPLOYABILITY SKILLS (10 MARKS)

UNIT NO.	NAME OF THE UNIT	OBJECTIVE TYPE QUESTIONS	SHORT ANSWER TYPE QUESTIONS	TOTAL QUESTIONS
		1 MARK EACH	2 MARKS EACH	
1	Communication Skills - II	1	1	2
2	Self-Management Skills - II	2	1	3
3	ICT Skills - II	1	1	2
4	Entrepreneurial Skills - II	1	1	2
5	Green Skills - II	1	1	2
	TOTAL QUESTIONS	6	5	11
	NO. OF QUESTIONS TO BE ANSWERED	Any 4	Any 3	07
	TOTAL MARKS	1 x 4 = 4	2 x 3 = 6	10 MARKS

PART B - SUBJECT SPECIFIC SKILLS (40 MARKS)

UNIT NO.	NAME OF THE UNIT	OBJECTIVE TYPE QUESTIONS	SHORT ANSWER TYPE QUESTIONS	DESCRIPTIVE/ LONG ANS. TYPE QUESTIONS	TOTAL QUESTIONS
		1 MARK EACH	2 MARKS EACH	4 MARKS EACH	
1	Digital Documentation (Advanced)	6	1	1	8
2	Electronic Spreadsheet (Advanced)	6	2	1	9
3	Database Management System	6	1	2	9
4	Maintain Health, Safety and Secure Working Environment	6	2	1	9
	TOTAL QUESTIONS	24	6	5	35
	NO. OF QUESTIONS TO BE ANSWERED	20	Any 4	Any 3	27
	TOTAL MARKS	1 x 20 = 20	2 x 4 = 8	4 x 3 = 12	40 MARKS

Preparation Assessment Zone

Welcome to the Preparation Assessment Zone !

In this section, you'll find **CBSE Sample Question Paper** and **Board Examination Paper 2024** to help you assess your readiness. Attempt these papers to familiarize yourself with the exam format and identify areas that need improvement.

Progress Tracker Tick the papers as you complete them.

- ☐ CBSE Sample Question Paper
- ☐ Board Examination Paper 2024

CBSE Sample Question Paper

Session 2024-25

Information Technology (Code 402)

Class 10

General Instructions

Time : 2 Hrs.

Max. Marks : 50

1. Please read the instructions carefully.
2. This Question Paper consists of 21 questions in two sections: Section A & Section B.
3. Section A has Objective Type Questions whereas Section B contains Subjective Type Questions.
4. Out of the given (5 + 16 = 21) questions, a candidate has to answer (5 + 10 = 15) questions in the allotted (maximum) time of 2 hours.
5. All questions of a particular section must be attempted in the correct order.
6. **Section A** Objective Type Questions (24 Marks)
   (i) This section has 5 questions.
   (ii) Marks allotted are mentioned against each question/part.
   (iii) There is no negative marking.
   (iv) Do as per the instructions given.
7. **Section B** Subjective Type Questions (26 Marks)
   (i) This section has 16 questions.
   (ii) A candidate has to do 10 questions.
   (iii) Do as per the instructions given.
   (iv) Marks allotted are mentioned against each question/part.

Section A Objective Type Questions *(24 Marks)*

1. Answer any 4 out of the given 6 questions based on Employability Skills (1 × 4 = 4)

(i) What is the importance of effective communication in a workplace?
(a) Reducing office expenses
(b) Enhancing team collaboration and productivity
(c) Increasing employee vacation days
(d) Improving office aesthetics

(ii) High expectations from self can leave with chronic anxiety and stress, thus leading to ____________ stress.
(a) Physical
(b) Emotional
(c) Social
(d) Financial

(iii) John notices that the cost of raw materials is lower in a different supplier's location compared to his current supplier. He decides to switch to the new supplier to save money.
Which function that the entrepreneur is doing?
(a) Makes decisions (b) Divides income
(c) Takes risk (d) Innovation

(iv) Imagine you are working on a challenging project for your studies, and you have a tight deadline. No one is around to cheer you on or offer encouragement, but you need to push through and complete the work.

What will make you complete work without others cheering you?

(a) Self-confidence (b) Communication
(c) Self-motivation (d) Self-esteem

(v) Which organization has adopted the Sustainable Development Goals.

(a) UNICEF
(b) League of Nations
(c) United Nations
(d) World Health Organization

(vi) What should you do to ensure secure online transactions?

(a) Lock your computer
(b) Give credit card or bank details only on safe websites
(c) Use anti-virus
(d) Do not use pirated software

2. Answer any 5 out of the given 6 questions (1 × 5 = 5)

(i) What is a style in LibreOffice Writer?

(a) A method of typing
(b) A collection of all formatting information
(c) A tool for drawing shapes
(d) A spell-check feature

(ii) Which of the following is an example for absolute cell referencing?

(a) C5 (b) C5
(c) $C (d) #C

(iii) Which of the following tabs is by default active when the Table of Contents, Entries or Bibliography dialog box is opened?

(a) Entries (b) Background
(c) Styles (d) Type

(iv) Which of the following is true about Track Changes feature of Writer?

(a) You cannot record a change made in the document.
(b) A comment of a particular author only can be deleted
(c) Any change made to the document is permanent.
(d) None of the above

(v) Imagine you are a financial analyst tasked with analyzing quarterly sales data for a multinational corporation. The data is stored in separate sheets within an Excel workbook, each representing sales figures from different regions (e.g., North Zone, East Zone, South Zone).

How can you efficiently view and compare quarterly sales data from multiple regions in a single spreadsheet to identify trends and relationships?

(a) By creating separate charts for each region's data.
(b) By using the Consolidate function to combine information from all regional sheets into one summary sheet.
(c) By manually copying and pasting data from each region's sheet into a new sheet.
(d) By deleting unnecessary data from each region's sheet.

(vi) Sore lower back is caused due to ____________.

(a) reaching forward frequently
(b) no lumbar support
(c) no upper back support from chair
(d) reaching forward for long periods

3. Answer any 5 out of the given 6 questions (1 × 5 = 5)

(i) What is the extension of spreadsheet file in Calc?

(a) .odb (b) .odt
(c) .odg (d) .ods

(ii) Which of the following is the shortcut key to open the Templates dialog box?

(a) Ctrl+Alt+N (b) Ctrl+Shift+N
(c) Ctrl+Alt+T (d) Shift+Alt+T

(iii) Which style category would you use to format a section containing text, graphics, and lists?

(a) Page Style (b) Paragraph Style
(c) Character Style (d) Frame Style

(iv) It is a reference point for the graphics which is created while positioning any image. This point could be the page, or frame where the object is either a paragraph, or even a character in a word processor.

(a) Wrap Text (b) Anchoring
(c) Alignment (d) BookMark

(v) Which of the following is an invalid Macro Name?

(a) 1formatword (b) format word
(c) format*word (d) Format_word

(vi) A fresh food cafeteria helps to maintain the ____________ of the employee.

(a) Health (b) Morale
(c) Productivity (d) Engagement

4. Answer any 5 out of the given 6 questions (1 × 5 = 5)

(i) Which of the following feature is used to jump to a different spreadsheet from the current spreadsheet in LibreOffice Calc?

(a) Macro (b) Hyperlink
(c) Connect (d) Copy

(ii) Which of the following operations cannot be performed using LibreOffice Calc?

(a) Store and manipulate data
(b) Create graphical representation of data
(c) Analysis of data
(d) Mail merge

(iii) The details associated with an entity are called ____________.

(a) Table (b) Attributes
(c) Records (d) Primary key

(iv) The ____________ data is a combination of letters, numbers or special characters.

(a) Structured (b) Unstructured
(c) Semi-structured (d) Alphanumeric

(v) Which kind of hazards can occur in IT industry?

(a) Biological (b) Chemical
(c) Physical (d) Ergonomic

(vi) In a Query Design wizard, which of the following buttons is clicked to move a field from 'Available fields' list box to 'Fields in the query' list box?

(a) > (b) < 9 (c) ∨ (d) ∧

5. Answer any 5 out of the given 6 questions (1 × 5 = 5)

(i) Identify the mode, where we can modify in the structure of table?

(a) Datasheet view (b) Structure view
(c) Design view (d) All of these

(ii) What is the primary purpose of a query in a database?

(a) To enter new records
(b) To create reports
(c) To retrieve specific data
(d) To design forms

(iii) Which of the following is NOT true about forms?

(a) It is the front end for data entry
(b) It can contain text fields
(c) Graphics can be inserted on the form
(d) It can accept only fixed number of records

(iv) For an organisation, the proper security procedures will reduce ____________.

(a) liabilities
(b) insurance
(c) business revenue
(d) operational charges of the company

(v) Which of the following is not an example of ignition sources of open flames?

(a) Gas ovens
(b) Lighters in smoking areas
(c) Welding torches
(d) Space heaters

(vi) Which action contributes to a healthy and safe working environment?

(a) Keeping emergency exits clear
(b) Leaving cables loose on the floor
(c) Ignoring safety warnings
(d) Using unapproved software

Section B Subjective Type Questions *(26 Marks)*

Answer any 3 out of the given 5 questions on Employability skills. Answer each question in 20-30 words. (2 × 3 = 6)

6. Imagine you are a high school student working on a group science project. You present your part of the project to your group, but you are not sure if it meets the expectations or aligns with what the group needs.

Why is it important for your classmates to give you feedback in this situation?

7. List the ways in which an entrepreneur affects a society.

8. Amit frequently experiences slow performance on his computer when working with large spreadsheets and multiple applications. He notices that the system

freezes and lags, especially when switching between programs.

What should Amit do to improve his computer's performance in handling large spreadsheets and multitasking?

9. How can you manage emotional intelligence?

10. How can individuals contribute to a sustainable future?

Answer any 4 out of the given 6 questions in 20-30 words each. (2 × 4 = 8)

11. Describe the steps to create a custom style named 'myStyle1' using drag-and-drop.

12. List and explain two common safety hazards in a workplace.

13. What is use of What-if Scenarios?

14. How do Merging and Comparing Spreadsheets differ in Calc?

15. Describe referential Integrity.

16. What causes eye strain and how to avoid it?

Answer any 3 out of the given 5 questions in 50-80 words each. (4 × 3 = 12)

17. Imagine you are preparing a series of school reports that need to include your school's logo, a picture of your project, and a standard footer with your name and class. Instead of adding and formatting these elements individually in each report, you use LibreOffice Writer templates to simplify this process.

(a) How can we apply the template from the available template list?

(b) When is exporting of templates useful?

18. Imagine you are a student organizing a fundraising event for your school club. You have a spreadsheet in LibreOffice Calc that lists donations from different sponsors. Each sponsor has contributed multiple times, and you need to summarize the total amount donated by each sponsor.

(a) Which tool in Calc can be used to create the group automatically?

(b) Which functions can be applied to the grouped data?

(c) Which menu option is used to apply this Tool?

(d) What is purpose of e (–)or (+) signs on grouped data?

19. What are Data Models? Explain different types of Data models.

20. Imagine you are a safety officer overseeing electrical maintenance work at a manufacturing plant. To spread the awareness among your team you have to conduct training on safety measures.

List out electrical rescue techniques which you will discuss with them.

21. Consider the following table: Employee

Emp_id	Name	Salary	Designation
E01	Kajal	78000	Manager
E02	Rahul	50000	Sales Executive
E03	Tarun	55000	Clerk

(a) You are tasked with designing a new employee database for your company. Based on the given table structure, identify the fields that would be necessary to store key information about each employee.

(b) As a database administrator, you need to ensure each employee has a unique identifier.

Which field in the table would you choose as the primary key, and why?

(c) During a review of the employee database, you realize there could be another field apart from the primary key that can uniquely identify a record. Identify the field and justify why it could serve as an alternate key.

(d) You are integrating the employee table with another table that stores department details.

Explain how you would use the primary key from the employee table and a foreign key in the department table to establish a relationship between the two tables. Illustrate with an example.

Answers in Topper's Style

1. (i) (b) (ii) (b) (iii) (a) (iv) (c) (v) (c) (vi) (b)
2. (i) (b) (ii) (b) (iii) (c) (iv) (b) (v) (b) (vi) (b)
3. (i) (d) (ii) (b) (iii) (d) (iv) (a) (v) (c) (vi) (a)
4. (i) (b) (ii) (d) (iii) (a) (iv) (b) (v) (d) (vi) (a)
5. (i) (c) (ii) (c) (iii) (d) (iv) (a) (v) (d) (vi) (a)
6. Feedback helps you determine whether your work meets group expectations, highlights areas for improvement, and ensures the project effectively achieves its objectives.
7. Entrepreneurs operate their businesses in a market where people buy and sell products and services. This exchange benefits everyone involved, as both buyers and sellers make money. Through this process, entrepreneurs contribute to the economic growth and development of their community and society.
8. When using a computer for an extended period, unnecessary files like temporary files and images accumulate, taking up valuable hard-disk space. This can reduce the computer's performance. To maintain efficiency, it's essential to regularly clean the system by deleting these extra files. Disk cleaner software can assist in this process by helping to remove unnecessary files.
9. Here are some steps to manage emotional intelligence:
   - **Understand your emotions** Pay attention to your behavior and identify areas for improvement. Once identified, focus on developing those aspects.
   - **Be rational** Avoid making impulsive decisions; think things through logically.
   - **Practice** Engage in meditation and yoga to help maintain calmness and emotional balance.
10. Individuals can help create a sustainable future by minimizing waste, conserving energy, choosing eco-friendly products, recycling, using sustainable transportation methods, and raising awareness about environmental issues to encourage responsible consumption and resource conservation.
11. Steps to Create a Custom Style Named 'myStyle1' Using Drag-and-Drop:
    (i) Open the Styles and Formatting sidebar in LibreOffice Writer.
    (ii) Right-click on an existing style similar to the desired 'myStyle1' or start with the default style.
    (iii) Adjust the formatting (e.g., font, size, color) using the toolbar or sidebar options.
    (iv) Drag the modified style and drop it into the 'Custom Styles' section in the Styles and Formatting sidebar to create 'myStyle1'.
12. (i) **Slips, Trips, and Falls** Result from wet floors, loose cables, or obstructed walkways.
    (ii) **Electrical Hazards** Caused by faulty wiring, overloaded circuits, or exposed electrical components.
13. What-if Analysis tool is used to explore and compare different alternatives under varying conditions. It is often employed at the start of a project to optimize results. By adjusting inputs and observing how they affect the outcome, the tool helps predict the best course of action for achieving the desired results.
14. Merging spreadsheets involves consolidating data from multiple sheets into one, often integrating information into a single source.

    Comparing spreadsheets focuses on analyzing differences between two sheets, identifying discrepancies in data or structure.
15. Referential integrity ensures the consistency of relationships between tables in a database. It requires that a foreign key in one table either matches a primary key in another table or is null, ensuring accurate and valid connections between related data.
16. **Potential Cause** Glares from overhead lights or windows, or incorrect glasses prescription needing a vision check.

    Precaution Adjust your desk and computer position so that light is not directly behind or in front of you.
17. (a) To apply the template from the available template list, follow the given steps"

    Step 1 Navigate to File > Templates > Manage Templates.

    Step 2 In the Templates dialog box, you'll see a list of available templates.

    Step 3 Choose the desired template and click the Open button. A new document will open with the name "Untitled," featuring the same content, appearance, and formatting as the selected template.

    Step 4 Make the necessary changes and save the file.

    (b) Exporting templates is beneficial for several reasons:
    - **Sharing Templates** Exporting enables you to distribute templates to colleagues or others

who need to use the same document formats, styles, or layouts.

- **Backing Up Templates** By creating backups, you safeguard your templates against software updates, changes, or potential data loss.
- **Transferring Templates** Exporting allows you to move templates between different computers or LibreOffice installations, maintaining consistency across various devices or users.

18. (a) In LibreOffice Calc, the tool used to automatically create groups is the Subtotals feature.

(b) The Subtotal tool in Calc automatically creates groups and applies common functions such as sum and average to the grouped data.

(c) Data>Subtotals option is used to apply Subtotals tool.

(d) Use the '+' sign to expand and the '–' sign to collapse the data.

19. A database can be structured in various ways depending on the type of data being stored. This structure is known as a data model, which outlines how data will be organized and accessed. A data model includes components for describing the data, the relationships between data, and the constraints governing the data. Here are some common data models:

Hierarchical Data Model In this model, data is organized into a tree-like structure.

Network Data Model This model links multiple records to the same master file, resembling an inverted tree where the master is at the bottom and the branches contain information linked to the master.

Relational Data Model This model is based on establishing relationships between two or more tables within a database. Data is stored in separate tables composed of rows and columns, and relationships are created using common fields across these tables. This is why it is called the relational database model.

20. The electrical rescue techniques are:

Approaching the Accident

- Avoid rushing into the accident scene.
- Immediately call emergency services (108).
- Approach the accident site with caution.

Examining the Scene

- Visually check if the victims are in contact with energized conductors.
- Be aware that metal surfaces or objects near the victim might be energized.
- Do not touch the victim or any conductive surfaces while they are energized.
- If possible, switch off the electrical circuits.

Hazards and Solutions

- Watch for hazards such as heated surfaces or fire.
- If you cannot turn off the power source, exercise extreme caution.
- Keep your hands and feet dry.
- Wear protective gear, including gloves and shoes, and stand on a clean, dry surface.
- Use non-conductive materials to remove the victim from the conductor.

High Voltage Rescue

- Rescuing victims in high voltage situations requires special training.
- Wear appropriate protective equipment, including gloves and shoes.

Applying First Aid

- Administer CPR if necessary.
- If the victim is breathing and has a heartbeat, provide first aid for injuries and treat for shock.
- Ensure the victim receives medical care promptly.
- Provide the attending physician with detailed information to facilitate accurate diagnosis and treatment.

21. (a) The fields are:
Emp_id, Name,Salary, Designation

(b) Emp_id

(c) Combination of Emp_id and Name

(d) Primary Key is the unique identifier for each row in a table. The filed designated as primary key cannot be NULL.

Example In the Employees table, the Emp_id serves as a foreign key. It establishes a relationship by linking to a primary key in another table. For instance, the Emp_id in the Orders table references the Emp_id in the Employees table.

Series **EF1GH/C**

Write your Roll No.

Board Examination Paper 2024

Information Technology 10th (Code 402)

No. of Ques : 21 | No. of Sections : 2 | Time : 2 Hrs. | Max. Marks : 50

General Instructions

1. Please read the instructions carefully.
2. This Question Paper consists of 21 questions in two sections: Section A & Section B.
3. Section A has Objective Type Questions whereas Section B contains Subjective Type Questions.
4. Out of the given (5 + 16 = 21) questions, a candidate has to answer (5 + 10 = 15) questions in the allotted (maximum) time of 2 hours.
5. All questions of a particular section must be attempted in the correct order.
6. **Section A** Objective Type Questions (24 Marks)
   (i) This section has 5 questions.
   (ii) There is no negative marking.
   (iii) Do as per the instructions given.
   (iv) Marks allotted are mentioned against each question/part.
7. **Section B** Subjective Type Questions (26 Marks)
   (i) This section has 16 questions.
   (ii) A candidate has to do 10 questions.
   (iii) Do as per the instructions given.
   (iv) Marks allotted are mentioned against each question/part.

Section A Objective Type Questions *(24 Marks)*

1. Answer any 4 out of the given 6 questions on Employability Skills. (4 × 1 = 4)

(i) The filename and filename extension are separated by a ....

(a) Dollar ($)
(b) Dot (.)
(c) Underscore (_)
(d) Hash (#)

(ii) Which of the following type of communication involves interchanging messages only through images or pictures?

(a) Verbal (b) Gesture
(c) Visual (d) Facial

(iii) ...... is the ability to identify and manage one's own emotion as well as the emotions of others.

(a) Self-Awareness
(b) Emotional Intelligence
(c) Stress Management
(d) Emotional Barrier

(iv) .... is the driving force that pushes us to achieve our goal, feel happy and improve our quality of life.

(a) Stress Management
(b) Self-Awareness
(c) Self-Growth
(d) Self-Motivation

(v) Which of the following is not an essential quality to become successful entrepreneur?

(a) Confidence (b) Creativity
(c) Patience (d) Wealthy

(vi) In total, how many SDGs were adopted by the United Nations 2015 as a universal call to action to end poverty, protect the planet and ensure that by 2030 all people enjoy peace and prosperity?

(a) 13 (b) 11
(c) 17 (d) 19

2. Answer any 5 out of the given 6 questions. $(5 \times 1 = 5)$

(i) Which of the following features allows one to apply a group of formats at the same time?

(a) Fill (b) Styles
(c) Images (d) Drag and Drop

(ii) In Writer, styles and formatting option is available under .... menu.

(a) Insert (b) Tools
(c) Format (d) Window

(iii) Gaurav is creating a report in Writer. The image gets embedded in his document whenever he drags and drops the image and the document size increases. Suggest a way to link the image file instead of embedding it.

(a) Drag and drop the image.
(b) Hold down the Ctrl key while dragging.
(c) Hold down the Shift key while dragging the image.
(d) Hold down the Ctrl and Shift key while dragging and dropping the image.

(iv) Resizing a .... may badly affect the resolution of an image.

(a) Vector image (b) Raster image
(c) CAD image (d) Coloured image

(v) In Writer, you can create your own template in .... way(s).

(a) One (b) Two
(c) Three (d) Four

(vi) In Writer, ... function key is used to see the databases while implementing mail merge.

(a) F1 (b) F2
(c) F3 (d) F4

3. Answer any 5 out of the given 6 questions: $(5 \times 1 = 5)$

(i) While consolidating data, a cell range can be named using .... option.

(a) Name range
(b) Define range
(c) Consolidate name
(d) Define name

(ii) Kawal and his friends are working on a Spreadsheet for entering data and updating records. They wish to keep a track of changes. Which of the following options will help in knowing who made the changes and what done in the spreadsheet?

(a) View changes (b) Record changes
(c) Store changes (d) Track changes

(iii) .... is a more elaborate form of Goal Seek.

(a) Database (b) Hyperlink
(c) Report (d) Solver

(iv) Macro functions can be written to behave as regular functions by writing a/an ....

(a) Void (b) Return
(c) Add-In (d) Dim

(v) .... option of Calc helps in viewing the changes made to a worksheet using original and edited worksheet.

(a) Edit → Revise document
(b) Edit → Consolidate
(c) Edit → Compare document
(d) Edit → Collaborate document

(vi) In Calc, shared workbooks allow

(a) Merging cells
(b) Conditional formatting
(c) Inserting pictures/graphs
(d) Adding text

4. Answer any 5 out of the given 6 questions. (5 × 1 = 5)

(i) In OpenOffice Base, the relationship applied on the tables can be removed with the help of .... option.
(a) Clear (b) Remove
(c) Drop (d) Delete

(ii) In SQL, the keyword to display records in ascending order is
(a) Asce (b) Incr
(c) Asc (d) High

(iii) .... is a numeric data type which can store Yes/No type values in the form of 0 or 1 in OpenOffice Base table.
(a) Boolean (b) Char
(c) Binary (d) OtherObject

(iv) Which of the following statement retrieves zero or more rows from one or more database tables or database views?
(a) UPDATE (b) DELETE
(c) SELECT (d) DISPLAY

(v) Roshni has created to table Customer in SQL and wants to store photograph image of every customer under Cust_photo field. Suggest a suitable data type from the options given below.
(a) IMAGE
(b) PICTURE
(c) LONGVARBINARY
(d) GRAPHIC

(vi) By default, all the fields in OpenOffice Base will have .... datatype.
(a) int (tiny)
(b) Boolean
(c) text (varchar)
(d) text (char)

5. Answer any 5 out of the given 6 questions. (5 × 1 = 5)

(i) A .... is a discussion style website similar to an online personal diary, used for creating personal web pages.
(a) WWW (b) Web
(c) Blog (d) Chat

(ii) Natasha works as floor manager. She has been assigned a task for conducting regular .... to ensure safety of life in case of any disaster or emergency by evacuating the place of danger.
(a) Cultural assembly
(b) Open house events
(c) Evacuation drill
(d) Trips and excursions

(iii) .... is an accessibility feature that assists people who have difficulty using a keyboard or a mouse (or both).
(a) Sticky keys (b) Serial key
(c) Control key (d) Toggle keys

(iv) Network in which all computers have equal status is called ....
(a) Peer-to-Peer architecture
(b) Central architecture
(c) Hierarchical architecture
(d) Client-server architecture

(v) .... are text files with small pieces of data; like a username and password.
(a) Operating System (b) Antivirus
(c) Cookies (d) Modem

(vi) DSL stands for ....
(a) Digital System Line
(b) Data Subscriber Line
(c) Digital Subscriber Line
(d) Data Service Line

Section B Subjective Type Questions *(26 Marks)*

Answer any 3 out of the given 5 questions on Employability Skills in 20-30 words each. (3 × 2 = 6)

6. How can cultural differences be a barrier to effective communication?

7. Explain any two misconceptions about entrepreneurship.

8. Briefly discuss the significance of time management skills in order to succeed in life.

9. Very often we hear about spam mails. Explain what are spam mails, and what should be done with such mails?

10. Mention any two ways to get clean and affordable energy.

Answer any 4 out of the given 6 questions in 20-30 words each. (4 × 2 = 8)

11. Write the main steps to group drawing objects in Writer.

12. What is the purpose of consolidating data in spreadsheets? Discuss briefly.

13. Differentiate between LAN and WAN.

14. What are the two parts of a cell reference while referencing data on other sheets? Explain with an example.

15. Give any two benefits of creating relationships between tables in a database.

16. Mention any two basic fire safety rules to be followed in any organisation.

Answer any 3 out of the given 4 questions in 50-80 words each. (3 × 4 = 12)

17. What is the concept of mail merge in word processing software? Discuss in detail. Also, give any two major benefits of using mail merge.

18. Explain four types of hyperlinks that can be applied in spreadsheets.

19. Internet security is of prime concern nowadays. Using strong passwords can lower the risk of security breach on the Internet. Himanshi has just created her first Internet based account. Help her by giving any four general guidelines for managing strong passwords.

20. In context of OpenOffice Base, explain the concept and significance of the following:

(a) Forms

(b) Reports

21. Consider the table Product and write SQL queries for the following:

Table : Product

PID	PNAME	PRICE	QUANTITY	CATEGORY
P01	BOARD	10000	2	OFFICE
P02	EYELINER	700	50	MAKEUP
P04	PENCIL	5	500	SCHOOL
P05	LAMP	250	10	DOMESTIC
P08	BEDSHEET	450	45	DOMESTIC
P09	LAPTOP	75000	15	OFFICE

(a) To display names of all products whose category is "DOMESTIC".

(b) To display product name and the price whose quantity is less than 50.

(c) To display price and quantity of LAPTOP.

(d) To display name and quantity of those products whose price is above 5000.

Answers in Topper's Style

1. (i) (b) The filename and filename extension are separated by a Dot (.)
   (ii) (c) Visual type of communication involves interchanging messages only through images or pictures.
   (iii) (b) Emotional Intelligence is the ability to identify and manage one's own emotion as well as the emotions of others.
   (iv) (d) Self-Motivation is the driving force that pushes us to achieve our goal, feel happy and improve our quality of life.
   (v) (d) Wealthy is not an essential quality to become successful entrepreneur.
   (vi) (c) In total, 17 SDGs were adopted by the United Nations 2015 as a universal call to action to end poverty, protect the planet and ensure that by 2030 all people enjoy peace and prosperity.
2. (i) (b) Styles features allows one to apply a group of formats at the same time.
   (ii) (c) In Writer, styles and formatting option is available under Format menu.
   (iii) (d) To link the file instead of embedding it, hold down the Ctrl+Shift keys while dragging and dropping the image.
   (iv) (b) Resizing a Raster image may badly affect the resolution of an image.
   (v) (b) In Writer, you can create your own template in two ways.
   (vi) (d) In Writer, F4 function key is used to see the database while implementing mail merge.
3. (i) (d) While consolidating data, a cell range can be named using Define name option.
   (ii) (d) To keep a track of changes, Track changes will help in knowing who made the changes and what changes were done in the spreadsheet.
   (iii) (d) Solver is a more elaborate form of Goal Seek.
   (iv) (b) Macro functions can be written to behave as regular functions by writing a Return.
   (v) (c) Edit → Compare document option of Calc helps in viewing the changes made to a worksheet using original and edited worksheet.
   (vi) (d) In Calc, shared workbooks allow Adding text.
4. (i) (d) The relationship applied on the tables can be removed also with the help of Delete option.
   (ii) (c) In SQL, the keyboard to display records in ascending order is Asc.
   (iii) (a) Boolean is a numeric data type which can store Yes/No type values in the form of 0 or 1 in OpenOffice Base table.
   (iv) (c) SELECT statement retrieves zero or more rows from one or more database tables or database views.
   (v) (c) LONGVARBINARY used to stores any array of byte (images, sounds, etc.).
   (vi) (c) By default, all the fields in OpenOffice Base will have text (varchar) datatype.
5. (i) (c) A Blog is a discussion style website similar to an online personal diary, used for creating personal web pages.
   (ii) (c) Evacuation drill is the process of emptying a place in case of an emergency or disaster.
   (iii) (b) Serial key is an accessibility feature that assists people that have difficulty in using a keyboard or a mouse or both.
   (iv) (a) Networks in which all computers have an equal status are called Peer to Peer networks.
   (v) (c) Cookies are text files that contain small pieces of data, like a username and password.
   (vi) (c) DSL stands for Digital Subscriber Line.
6. Cultural differences can lead to misunderstandings and confusion, making it hard to communicate clearly and effectively with others.
7. (i) **Starting a Business is Easy** In reality, it is a very difficult and challenging process to start a successful business. The rate of failure of new ventures is very high but small entrepreneurships are comparatively easier to start.
   (ii) **Lot of Money to Finance New Business** Successful entrepreneurs design their business with little cash also.
8. Time management is crucial for success, helping prioritise tasks, reduce stress, meet deadlines, and achieve goals efficiently and effectively.
9. Spam mails are unwanted emails, often promoting scams or irrelevant content. They should be deleted or marked as spam.
10. Two ways to get clean and affordable energy are:
    1. **Solar power** Using sunlight to generate electricity through solar panels, which is clean and affordable in the long term.
    2. **Wind power** Utilising wind turbines to convert wind energy into electricity, providing a clean and cost-effective energy source.
11. The main steps to group drawing objects in Writer are:
    1. Select the drawing objects you want to group.
    2. Right-click on any of the selected objects.

3. Choose "Group" from the menu that appears.
4. Now, you can move and resize them together.

12. Consolidating data in spreadsheets helps organise, summarise, and analyse information from multiple sources in one place, making it easier to understand trends, make decisions, and findings communicate effectively.

13.

LAN (Local Area Network)	WAN (Wide Area Network)
Small geographic area	Large geographic area
High speed	Slower compared to LAN
Privately owned or controlled	Public or private ownership
Home, office networks	Internet, global networks

14. In Calc, a cell reference for data on other sheets consists of the sheet name and the cell address.

Example 'Sheet2.A1' refers to cell A1 on Sheet2.

15. Two benefits of creating relationships between tables in a database are:

1. **Efficient data retrieval** Relationships help in fetching related information quickly without redundancy.
2. **Data integrity** Relationships enforce consistency, preventing errors and ensuring accurate data storage and retrieval.

16. (i) Keep workplace a no-smoking zone.
(ii) Fire escape plans must be installed at proper levels.

17. Mail merge is a feature in word processing software that combines a template document with a data source, like a list of names and addresses, to create personalised documents, such as letters or emails. It automates the process of customising multiple documents, saving time and reducing errors.

Two major benefits include:

1. **Efficiency** It eliminates the need for manual copying and pasting of individual data into each document.
2. **Personalisation** It allows for customisation of documents for each recipient, enhancing communication effectiveness.

18. Four types of hyperlinks that can be applied in spreadsheets are as follows:

1. **URL Hyperlinks** Direct links to websites or online resources.
2. **Document Hyperlinks** Links to other documents or files on your computer.
3. **Email Hyperlinks** Links that open a new email with a pre-defined recipient.
4. **Sheet Navigation Hyperlinks** Links that take you to a specific cell or sheet within the same spreadsheet.

Each type allows users to access different kinds of information or actions quickly and conveniently within a spreadsheet.

19. Four general guidelines for managing strong passwords are:

1. **Complexity** Create passwords with a mix of uppercase and lowercase letters, numbers, and special characters.
2. **Length** Longer passwords are harder to crack, so aim for at least 12 characters.
3. **Unique** Avoid using the same password for multiple accounts to prevent an effect, if one is compromised.
4. **Avoid Predictability** Don't use easily guessable information like birthdays or pet names. Instead, think of a random phrase or use a password manager for secure storage.

20. (a) **Forms** In OpenOffice Base, forms are like digital paper versions, where you can input or edit data into your database. They make it easier to enter information in an organised way, like filling out a form at a doctor's office.

(b) **Reports** Reports, help you present your data in a neat and understandable format. They summarise and analyse the information stored in your database, making it easier to understand trends or patterns, similar to a summary report you might get after a survey.

21. (a) `SELECT PNAME FROM Product WHERE CATEGORY = 'DOMESTIC';`

(b) `SELECT PNAME, PRICE FROM Product WHERE QUANTITY < 50;`

(c) `SELECT PRICE, QUANTITY FROM Product WHERE PNAME = 'LAPTOP';`

(d) `SELECT PNAME, QUANTITY FROM Product WHERE PRICE > 5000;`

Proficiency Building Zone

Welcome to the Proficiency Building Zone !

This section contains **10 Sample Question Papers** designed to enhance your problem-solving skills and proficiency. Use these papers to practice regularly and track your progress. Remember, consistent practice is key to mastering Information Technology.

Progress Tracker Tick the papers as you complete them.

- [ ] Sample Paper 1 _____ (Fill your score)
- [ ] Sample Paper 2 _____ (Fill your score)
- [ ] Sample Paper 3 _____ (Fill your score)
- [ ] Sample Paper 4 _____ (Fill your score)
- [ ] Sample Paper 5 _____ (Fill your score)
- [ ] Sample Paper 6 _____ (Fill your score)
- [ ] Sample Paper 7 _____ (Fill your score)
- [ ] Sample Paper 8 _____ (Fill your score)
- [ ] Sample Paper 9 _____ (Fill your score)
- [ ] Sample Paper 10 _____ (Fill your score)

SQP Code : **PB-1/10** Series *i*-**Succeed 1-25/10** Roll No.

Sample Question Paper 01

Information Technology 10th (Code 402)

General Instructions

Time : 2 Hrs.

Max. Marks : 50

1. Please read the instructions carefully.
2. This Question Paper consists of 21 questions in two sections: Section A & Section B.
3. Section A has Objective Type Questions whereas Section B contains Subjective Type Questions.
4. Out of the given (5 + 16 = 21) questions, a candidate has to answer (5 + 10 = 15) questions in the allotted (maximum) time of 2 hours.
5. All questions of a particular section must be attempted in the correct order.
6. **Section A** Objective Type Questions (24 Marks)
   (i) This section has 5 questions.
   (ii) Marks allotted are mentioned against each question/part.
   (iii) There is no negative marking.
   (iv) Do as per the instructions given.
7. **Section B** Subjective Type Questions (26 Marks)
   (i) This section has 16 questions.
   (ii) A candidate has to do 10 questions.
   (iii) Do as per the instructions given.
   (iv) Marks allotted are mentioned against each question/part.

Section A Objective Type Questions *(24 Marks)*

1. Answer any 4 out of the given 6 questions based on Employability Skills. $(4 \times 1 = 4)$

(i) High expectations from self can leave one with chronic anxiety and stress, thus leading to .... stress.

(a) physical (b) emotional
(c) mental (d) financial

(ii) Which term means walking in the local park or a similar activity?

(a) Nature walk
(b) Motivation
(c) Regulation
(d) None of the above

(iii) It is a picture or graphic representation of an application or a file.

(a) Icon (b) Taskbar
(c) Status bar (d) Desktop

(iv) A/An .... creates new needs and new means to satisfy them.

(a) leadership (b) innovation
(c) entrepreneur (d) None of these

(v) Non-verbal communication includes

(a) Written messages
(b) Facial expressions
(c) Email communication
(d) Phone calls

(vi) Which of the following is not a solution for sustainable development?
(a) Education and awareness programs
(b) Sustainable agriculture practices
(c) Deforestation and habitat destruction
(d) Green technology advancements

2. Answer any 5 out of the given 6 questions. (5 × 1 = 5)

(i) A template is a model that you use to create ....
(a) images (b) other documents
(c) design (d) DBMS

(ii) Which of the following is a set of formats consisting of such things as fonts, colors etc?
(a) Style (b) Margin
(c) Indent (d) Leading

(iii) Which extension is given to a document by default in LibreOffice writer?
(a) .odf (b) .com
(c) .docx (d) None of these

(iv) In a document, ... is used to apply a style to many different areas quickly without having to go back to the Styles and Formatting window and double click every time.
(a) Fill format mode
(b) Formatting window
(c) Painter mode
(d) Text wrapping

(v) Tanu explained her class that to apply an existing style, except for ...., position the insertion point in the paragraph, frame or page and then double-click on the name of the style in one of these lists.
(a) Window style (b) Character style
(c) Paragraph style (d) Cell style

(vi) In a document, ... refers to the vertical or horizontal placement of a graphic in relation to the chosen anchor point.
(a) arrangement (b) alignment
(c) identation (d) margin

3. Answer any 5 out of the given 6 questions. (5 × 1 = 5)

(i) Which function cannot be performed through Subtotal in a Spreadsheet?
(a) Sum (b) Product
(c) Average (d) Percentage

(ii) It refers to a cell or a range of cells on a worksheet and can be used to find a formula.
(a) Row (b) Column
(c) Autosum (d) Cell reference

(iii) The .... feature creates a summarized outline of data in a worksheet.
(a) Subtotal (b) Solver
(c) Goal Seek (d) Scenario

(iv) Raj has created a worksheet where he has added all the information of his employees. He wants every employee to go through the worksheet and update their address and phone number, if required. He also would like to know the changes done by his employees. Which feature of spreadsheet he should enable to see the changes made by his employees?
(a) Macro
(b) Link workbook
(c) Change worksheet
(d) Track changes

(v) One can create a report based on a table or a ________ or both.
(a) Fields (b) Memo
(c) Query (d) Datatype

(vi) To copy a formula from one cell to another
(a) Drag the autofill handle
(b) Cut the cell
(c) Both (a) and (b)
(d) None of the above

4. Answer any 5 out of the given 6 questions. (5 × 1 = 5)

(i) Facilities offered by databases are
(a) the ability to store a large amount of data in a structured format, easy

SP-01

update, sort query, production of reports.
(b) easy edition, spell check, perform calculations, library of mathematical functions, replication.
(c) the ability to rotate images, copy and paste, fill scale.
(d) None of the above

(ii) Computer based record keeping system is known as
(a) Data Manipulation System
(b) Computerised Data System
(c) Computerised Record Keeping System
(d) DBMS

(iii) Database servers are referred to as
(a) front-ends (b) back-ends
(c) clients (d) model

(iv) Which of the following is not a data type?
(a) Picture/Graphic (b) Date/Time
(c) Text (d) Number

(v) When you define a field for a table, ... are the names given to column in a table.
(a) Field Name (b) Field Size
(c) Data Type (d) Description

(vi) Which of the following commands is not a data manipulation language?
(a) Select (b) Insert
(c) Update (d) Alter

5. Answer any 5 out of the given 6 questions $(5 \times 1 = 5)$

(i) What does the Hazard Communication Standard (HCS) require employers to do?
(a) Provide safety training only to supervisors
(b) Keep safety data sheets (SDS) confidential
(c) Label hazardous chemicals properly
(d) Exclude temporary workers from safety protocols

(ii) This sign is used to alert people for

(a) Wet floor (b) Wet ceiling
(c) Do not run (d) Do not jump

(iii) What is the primary purpose of an evacuation drill?
(a) To test the fire alarm system
(b) To practice emergency response procedures
(c) To assess employee fitness levels
(d) To evaluate workplace cleanliness

(iv) Materials such as wood, cloth, and paper, which won't ignite on their own but will continue to burn once exposed to a heat source. Under which category these materials fall?
(a) Class D (b) Class C
(c) Class B (d) Class A

(v) A .... is a location or a place of employment, where someone works to earn his living.
(a) Workplace (b) Home
(c) Society (d) Industry

(vi) Repetitive use of muscle may feel pain in your ___________.
(a) neck (b) shoulder
(c) wrist or fingers (d) All of these

SP-01

Section B Subjective Type Questions *(26 Marks)*

Answer any 3 out of the given 5 questions on Employability Skills. Answer each question in 20-30 words. $(3 \times 2 = 6)$

6. When interviewing job candidates, what qualities do employers find impressive?

7. What do you mean by internal stress?

8. What are the facilities provided by operating system?

9. Explain innovativeness as a quality of entrepreneur.

10. What policies can support the development of green skills?

Answer any 4 out of the given 6 questions in 20-30 words each. (4 × 2 = 8)

11. Explain the role of template in word processor.
12. What is the significance of consolidate in Calc?
13. Write down the significance of electronic spreadsheets.
14. When is Memo data type is preferred over Text data type for a field?
15. What are slipping and tripping hazards?
16. In context to emergency explain the use of first-aid.

Answer any 3 out of the given 5 questions in 50-80 words each. (3 × 4 = 12)

17. How can a document's style be changed? Explain with proper steps.
18. Arihant stationery keeps stock of various stationeries in his shop. The proprietor wants to maintain a stock value and reorder level for following items as given in a spreadsheet. Write formulas for the operation (i) to (iii) and answer the question (iv) based on the spreadsheet given below along with the relevant cell address.

	A	B	C	D	E	F	G	H
1	Item Code	Item Name	Minimum Stock Quantity	Quantity in Stock (Unit)	Rate (₹)	Stock Value (₹)	Quantity to Order (Unit)	Order Value
2	101	P. Holder	200	500	35			
3	123	Whitner	450	150	25			
4	113	Steppler Pin	250	450	5			
5	156	Paper cutter	300	600	10			

Sheet1 Sheet2 Sheet3

(i) To calculate the Stock Value as product of 'Quantity in Stock' and 'Rate' for each item present in the spreadsheet.

(ii) To calculate the 'Quantity to Order' as 'Minimum Stock Quantity'-'Quantity in Stock' for each item.

(iii) To calculate the 'Order Value' as product of 'Quantity to Order' and 'Rate' for the items if 'Quantity to Order' > = 0, else assign the value as 0.

(iv) Proprietor wants to graphically represent his stationery stock. Suggest him the most appropriate feature of MS-Excel.

19. Consider the following table: Employee

Table : Employee

Emp_no	E_name	Profile	Manager	Hire_date	Salary	Commission	Dept_no
8369	SMITH	CLERK	8902	1990-12-18	8000	NULL	20
8499	ANYA	SALESMAN	8698	1991-02-20	16000	300.00	30
8521	SETH	SALESMAN	8698	1991-02-22	12500	500.00	30
8566	MAHADEVAN	MANAGER	8839	1991-04-02	29850	NULL	20
8654	MOMIN	SALESMAN	8698	1991-09-28	12500	1400.00	30
8698	BINA	MANAGER	8839	1991-05-01	28500	NULL	30

(a) How many fields and records are there in the table Employee?

(b) Write the SQL queries for the following:

(i) Display E_name and salary of those employees whose Salary is less than or equal to 16000.

(ii) Display details of employees who are getting commission of ₹ 300 or greater.

(iii) Display all the details of the employee profile 'CLERK'.

20. Ajay is learning about the different terms and commands of a database. He came across the following terms . Tell him the definition of the following

(i) Insert command

(ii) Select command

(iii) Delete command

(iv) DCL command

21. You are in an office building when you notice smoke coming from a wastebasket in the corner of the room. The fire is small but spreading quickly. You see a fire extinguisher mounted on the wall nearby.

What steps should you take to properly and safely use the fire extinguisher to put out the fire?

Answers *in Topper's Style*

My Commitment *I affirm that I am reviewing these solutions only after I have solved the Sample Question Paper 1 on my own. My purpose of looking the solutions is solely to verify whether my answers/solutions were correct or not and to identify my mistakes in case my solutions were wrong or I could not solve that.*

1. (i) (c) (ii) (a) (iii) (a) (iv) (b) (v) (b) (vi) (c)

2. (i) (b) (ii) (a) (iii) (d) (iv) (a) (v) (b) (vi) (b)

3. (i) (d) (ii) (d) (iii) (a) (iv) (d) (v) (c) (vi) (a)

4. (i) (a) (ii) (d) (iii) (b) (iv) (a) (v) (a) (vi) (d)

5. (i) (c) (ii) (a) (iii) (b) (iv) (d) (v) (a) (vi) (d)

6. During a personal interview, employers are impressed by a job candidate with the qualities of answering questions with more than one-word answers, demonstrating that he is listening and sharing information and ideas by asking questions for clarification and follow-up.

7. Internal stress generates within the humans regarding unreasonable matters. This internal stress is one of the most important kinds of stress to understand and manage because it keeps on building up as time passes. For example, some people become used to the kind of hurried, tense, lifestyle of persons living in large cities.

8. The facilities provided by operating system are:
   - Easy interaction between humans and computers.
   - Starting computer automatically when power is turned ON.
   - Loading and scheduling users' programs along with necessary compilers.
   - Controlling Input and Output.

9. With the changing needs and requirements of customers production should meet requirements with the help of innovative ideas. An entrepreneurial venture does not have to restrict itself to just one innovation or even one type of innovation. Success can be built on combination of innovation for example, a new product delivered in a new way with a new message.

10. Policies such as funding incentives, vocational training programs, and partnerships between educational institutions and industries can foster the development and utilization of green skills.

11. In word processor, templates are a special type of document that can hold text, styles, macros, keyboard shortcuts, custom toolbars, QAT and ribbon modifications and building blocks including Auto Text entries.

12. Consolidate is a function used to combine information from multiple sheets of the spreadsheet into one place to summarize the information. It is used to view and compare variety of data in a single spreadsheet for identifying trends and relationships.

13. Using electronic spreadsheets, large volume of data can be stored in worksheets. Worksheets can be managed, edited, viewed, retrieved and printed easily in desired format. Electronic spreadsheets support charts, which represent data pictorically.

14. Text data type is not capable to store the project description because its length cannot be more than 255 characters so, Memo data type is preferred over Text data type.

15. You slip when you lose your footing whereas you trip when you catch your foot on or in something and you fall when you come down suddenly wet or oily surfaces, occasional spills, flooring that do not have same degree of fraction in all areas etc are common causes of slips whereas trip occurs due to wrinkled carpeting, poor lighting, obstructed view, uncovered cables, ladders etc.

16. First aid should be quickly accessible to the employees at the workplace. It should contain all the important items for first aid required to deal with common problems such as cuts, burns, headaches and muscle cramps.

17. You can change an existing style in style gallery in two ways

1. To change an existing style using the Style dialog, right-click on the required style in the Styles and Formatting window and select **Modify** from the pop-up menu.

   The Style dialog displayed depends on the type of style selected. Each style dialog has several tabs.

2. To change a style from a selection:

   Step 1 Open the Styles and Formatting dialog.

   Step 2 In the document, select an item that has the format you want to adopt as a style.

   Step 3 In the Styles and Formatting dialog, select the style you want to update (single-click, not double-click), then long-click on the arrow next to the New Style from Selection icon and click on Update Style.

18. (i) At cell F2, type = D2*E2 and then copy this formula using Fill handle in range F3 : F5.

(ii) At cell G2, type = C2-D2 and then copy this formula using Fill handle in range G3 : G5.

(iii) At cell H2, type = IF (G2 > = 0, G2*E2, 0) and copy this formula using Fill handle in the range H3 : H5.

(iv) He should create chart of any type to graphically represent his data.

19. (a) There are 8 fields and 6 records in the table Employee.

Common Mistake

Students always get confused between records and fields. They consider number of columns as records of any Table. While records are rows and attributes or fields are columns.

(b) (i)
```
SELECT E_name, Salary FROM Employee
WHERE Salary< = 16000;
```

(ii)
```
SELECT* FROM Employee WHERE Commission >
= 300;
```

(iii)
```
SELECT *FROM Employee WHERE
Profile="CLERK";
```

20. (i) **INSERT Command** It is used to add a single record or multiple records into a table.

Syntax

```
INSERT INTO <table_name> (col1, col2.....)
VALUES (val1, val2);
```

(ii) **SELECT Command** It is used to query or retrieve data from a table in the database.

Syntax

```
SELECT column_list FROM table_name WHERE
<condition>;
```

(iii) **DELETE Command** To discard unwanted data from a database, the delete command is used.

Syntax

```
DELETE FROM <table_name> WHERE <condition>;
```

(iv) **DCL Command** These commands are used to assign security levels in database which involves multiple user setups.

They are used to grant defined role and access privileges to the users.

e.g. GRANT and REVOKE command.

21. Steps to properly and safely fire extinguisher are:

Step 1 Identify the safety pin of the fire extinguisher, present in its handle.

Step 2 Break the seal and pull the safety pin from the handle.

Step 3 Use the fire extinguisher by squeezing the lever.

Step 4 Sweep it from side to side.

SQP Code : **PB-2/10** Series ***i*-Succeed 2-25/10** Roll No.

Sample Question Paper 02

Information Technology 10th (Code 402)

General Instructions

Time : 2 Hrs.

Max. Marks : 50

1. Please read the instructions carefully.
2. This Question Paper consists of 21 questions in two sections: Section A & Section B.
3. Section A has Objective Type Questions whereas Section B contains Subjective Type Questions.
4. Out of the given (5 + 16 = 21) questions, a candidate has to answer (5 + 10 = 15) questions in the allotted (maximum) time of 2 hours.
5. All questions of a particular section must be attempted in the correct order.
6. **Section A** Objective Type Questions (24 Marks)
   (i) This section has 5 questions.
   (ii) Marks allotted are mentioned against each question/part.
   (iii) There is no negative marking.
   (iv) Do as per the instructions given.
7. **Section B** Subjective Type Questions (26 Marks)
   (i) This section has 16 questions.
   (ii) A candidate has to do 10 questions.
   (iii) Do as per the instructions given.
   (iv) Marks allotted are mentioned against each question/part.

Section A Objective Type Questions *(24 Marks)*

1. Answer any 4 out of the given 6 questions based on Employability Skills. $(4 \times 1 = 4)$

(i) Which one of the following is not a symptom of stress?
(a) Increased sweating
(b) Dry mouth
(c) Cold hands or feet
(d) None of the above

(ii) Which term refers to our knowledge and understanding of ourselves?
(a) Self-awareness
(b) Motivation
(c) Both (a) and (b)
(d) None of the above

(iii) Which of the following is an example of effective written communication?
(a) Using excessive jargon and technical terms
(b) Writing lengthy paragraphs without any breaks or bullet points
(c) Using concise and clear language
(d) Including personal opinions and biases

(iv) .... provides process and memory management services that allow two or more tasks, jobs or programs to run simultaneously.
(a) Multi-tasking (b) Multi-threading
(c) Multi-processing (d) Multi-computing

(v) Which of the following is an example of a green skill?
(a) Traditional farming techniques
(b) Renewable energy installation and maintenance
(c) Conventional manufacturing processes
(d) Non-recyclable waste disposal methods

(vi) In which situation an entrepreneur will not be able to convince his fellow beings to achieve his goals?
(a) Low self-confidence
(b) Innovativeness
(c) Risk-taking
(d) None of the above

2. Answer any 5 out of the given 6 questions. (5 × 1 = 5)

(i) Which of the following is not an AutoShape?
(a) Line (b) Circle
(c) Curve (d) ClipArt

(ii) Editing Custom Shapes feature allows ...... of small segments of a drawing.
(a) shaping (b) reshaping
(c) rehearse (d) None of these

(iii) Template includes a text space that is surrounded by brackets. It is called a ....
(a) margin
(b) placeholder
(c) data source
(d) track changes

(iv) A _____ is a document model that you use to create other documents.
(a) Anchoring (b) Alignment
(c) Template (d) None of these

(v) Which of the following alignment aligns the text along with the page margin?
(a) Left
(b) Center
(c) Justify
(d) Along margin

(vi) Suraj wants to know the sequence of steps used to open the Templates dialog. Answer to his query.
(a) File → New → Text Document
(b) File → New → Templates
(c) Format → Group → Group
(d) None of the above

3. Answer any 5 out of the given 6 questions. (5 × 1 = 5)

(i) Which of the following allows you to reorder data?
(a) Sorting (b) Filtering
(c) Scenario (d) Custom sorting

(ii) Neeta is planning to take a car loan to buy a new car. But she is not sure about the payback time, i.e. whether to pay it back in 5 or 6 years considering that her monthly fuel cost will also increase. In such cases, which of the following features of spreadsheet can she use to get an idea about it?
(a) Consolidation (b) Macros
(c) Templates (d) What-if analysis

(iii) What is the name given to a combination of two cell references?
(a) Relative reference
(b) Absolute reference
(c) Mixed reference
(d) None of the above

(iv) Which of the following operations cannot be performed using LibreOffice Calc?
(a) Store and manipulate data
(b) Create graphical representation of data
(c) Analysis of data
(d) Mail merge

(v) Which of the following allows you to display the specific data?
(a) Arranging
(b) Filtering
(c) Scenario
(d) Custom sorting

(vi) The default page orientation in spreadsheet is
(a) Landscape
(b) Horizontal
(c) Portrait
(d) None of these

4. Answer any 5 out of the given 6 questions. (5 × 1 = 5)

(i) The ………… SQL statement is used to make a query or retrieve data from a table in a database.
(a) INSERT (b) UPDATE
(c) SELECT (d) REVIEW

(ii) DBMS is a program, that controls the creation, maintenance and use of a database. Here, DBMS stands for
(a) Digital Base Management System
(b) Data Build Management System
(c) Database Management System
(d) Database Management Service

(iii) Key field is a unique identifier for each record. It is defined in the form of ______.
(a) rows (b) columns
(c) tree (d) query

(iv) 1:1, 1:n and n:1 are examples of different types of _______ .
(a) Relations (b) Databases
(c) Data (d) Query

(v) Rajiv has created an employee table and made Emp_No, as the primary key, so that it can accept only unique values for each record. At the same time, he wants to have one more field that can behave like a primary key. Which of the following types of key can serve the purpose?
(a) Foreign key (b) Composite key
(c) Unique key (d) None of these

(vi) ______is used to define the structure of your tables and other objects in the database.
(a) DDL (b) DML
(c) DCL (d) None of these

5. Answer any 5 out of the given 6 questions. (5 × 1 = 5)

(i) What is the primary fire emergency telephone number is?
(a) 011
(b) 101
(c) 108
(d) 111

(ii) Sore lower back is caused due to ____________.
(a) reaching forward frequently
(b) no lumbar support
(c) no upper back support from chair
(d) reaching forward for long periods

(iii)

Look at the image and identify under which of the following category of hazards it falls into?
(a) Safety (b) Physical
(c) Biological (d) Chemical

(iv) The proper security procedures will increase ____________.
(a) liabilities
(b) insurance
(c) business revenue
(d) operational charges of the company

(v) A company should have at least ……… exit routes for proper evacuation during an emergency.
(a) 1 (b) 2
(c) 4 (d) Not required

(vi) Which of the following is an examples of ignition sources of open flames?
(a) Gas ovens
(b) Lighters in smoking areas
(c) Welding torches
(d) All of the above

Section B Subjective Type Questions *(26 Marks)*

Answer any 3 out of the given 5 questions on Employability Skills. (3 × 2 = 6)

Answer each question in 20-30 words.

6. How stress can be caused by both good and bad experiences?
7. How do green skills contribute to sustainable development?
8. What is the difference between moving and copying a folder?
9. How entrepreneur is helpful in capital formation?
10. Can you explain what it means to encode a message?

Answer any 4 out of the given 6 questions in 20-30 words each. (4 × 2 = 8)

11. What is the use of grouping objects in a word processor application?
12. What is the difference between a workbook and worksheet?
13. What is the use of Scenario tool?
14. Define data, the major component of a database.
15. List out any two electrical rescue techniques.
16. Explain any two ways to reduce musculoskeletal problems.

Answer any 3 out of the given 5 questions in 50-80 words each. (3 × 4 = 12)

17. What is sorting? How to use ascending or descending sort which depends on one column?
18. Ojas had prepared a Table of Contents of the project work he had done in a word processor application.
    (a) Tell him the different steps to update the TOC.
    (b) Tell him the different steps to delete the TOC.
19. Consider the following table: Employee

Table : Employee

Emp_no	E_name	Profile	Manager	Hire_date	Salary	Commission	Dept_no
8369	SMITH	CLERK	8902	1990-12-18	8000	NULL	20
8499	ANYA	SALESMAN	8698	1991-02-20	16000	300.00	30
8521	SETH	SALESMAN	8698	1991-02-22	12500	500.00	30
8566	MAHADEVAN	MANAGER	8839	1991-04-02	29850	NULL	20
8654	MOMIN	SALESMAN	8698	1991-09-28	12500	1400.00	30
8698	BINA	MANAGER	8839	1991-05-01	28500	NULL	30

(a) How many fields and records are there in the table Employee?

(b) Write the SQL queries for the following:

(i) Display E_name and Salary of those employees whose Salary is greater than or equal to 22000.

(ii) Display details of employees those are not getting Commission.

(iii) Display all the details of the employee profile 'SALESMAN'.

20. Define the following types of integrity :
    (i) Entity integrity
    (ii) Domain integrity
    (iii) Referential integrity
    (iv) User defined integrity
21. Sunil, a software developer, spends long hours working at his desk. Lately, he's been experiencing back pain and wrist strain. What ergonomic adjustments should he consider to alleviate these issues?

SP-02

Answers in Topper's Style

My Commitment *I affirm that I am reviewing these solutions only after I have solved the Sample Question Paper 2 on my own. My purpose of looking the solutions is solely to verify whether my answers/solutions were correct or not and to identify my mistakes in case my solutions were wrong or I could not solve that.*

1. (i) (d) (ii) (a) (iii) (c) (iv) (a) (v) (b) (vi) (a)
2. (i) (d) (ii) (b) (iii) (b) (iv) (c) (v) (c) (vi) (b)
3. (i) (a) (ii) (d) (iii) (c) (iv) (d) (v) (b) (vi) (c)
4. (i) (c) (ii) (c) (iii) (b) (iv) (a) (v) (b) (vi) (a)
5. (i) (b) (ii) (b) (iii) (a) (iv) (c) (v) (b) (vi) (d)
6. Stress can be caused by both good and bad experiences like when people feel stressed by something going on around them, their bodies react by releasing chemicals into the blood.

   These chemicals give more energy and strength, which can be a good thing if their stress is caused by physical danger but it can also be a bad thing, if the stress is in response to something emotional and there is no outlet for this extra energy and strength. The good stress is called eustress, whereas the bad stress is termed as distress.
7. Green skills enable the transition to a more sustainable society by promoting responsible resource management, reducing pollution, and fostering social and economic well-being.
8. Differences between moving and copying a folder are as follows

Copying a Folder	Moving a Folder
Copying a folder means to make a duplicate copy of a folder.	Moving a folder means to transfer a folder from one location to another.
It uses Copy and Paste option.	It uses Cut and Paste option.
The original folder remains at the source location.	The original folder is moved to the destination location.

9. An entrepreneur is helpful in capital formation as we know that increase in the rate of capital formation is quite essential for the economic development of any country. Those nations which are not able to increase the rate of capital formation or does it nominally remain backward from industrial development's point of view.
10. Encoding a message means to change the message into a form suitable for sending. The factors which must be considered when encoding messages are language, cultural differences etc.
11. Grouping drawing objects make it easier to handle several objects as a single entity, while preserving their relative sizes and positions. When objects are grouped, any editing operations carried out on that group are applied to all members of the group. If you click on one member of the group, the whole group is selected.
12. Differences between workbook and worksheet are as follows:

Workbook	Worksheet
A workbook is an Excel file with one or more worksheets	A worksheet is a single spreadsheet of data.
A workbook would be the entire binder, with everything in it.	A worksheet would be like one section in that binder.

13. A Scenario is a set of values that Calc saves for a group of cells. Whenever we run a scenario, Calc automatically substitutes the saved cell values into a connected formula to give us an output. By having different scenarios for a same group of cells we can get different results from the formula and compare these results to know which is the most suitable set of values for us.
14. Data is raw numbers, characters or facts represented by a value. Most of the organisations generate, store and process large amounts of data. The data acts as a bridge between the hardware and the software. Data may be of different types such as User data, Metadata and Application Metadata.
15. Two electrical rescue techniques are:
    - Never rush into an accident situation.
    - Call 108 as soon as possible.
    - Approach the accident place cautiously.
16. To avoid this problem,
    - Position your computer such that the end of the monitor should be at your eye level.
    - Keep the neck neutral with monitor directly ahead to prevent to turn your neck.
    - Keep your monitor at least arm length distance, or 20 to 30 inch away from you.
17. Sorting is a common spreadsheet task that allows user to easily re-order the data. The most common type of sorting is alphabetical ordering which you can do in ascending or descending order.

    To use ascending or descending sort which depends on one column, follow the given steps:

Highlight the cells to be sorted, then select Data → Sort to open the Sort dialog, or click the Sort Ascending or Sort Descending toolbar buttons. Using the dialog, you can sort the selected cells using up to three columns, in either ascending (A-Z, 1-9) or descending (Z-A, 9-1) order.

18. Writer does not update the table of contents automatically, so after any changes to the headings, you must update it manually.

(a) To update a table of contents when changes are made to the document:

(i) Right-click anywhere in the TOC.

(ii) From the pop-up menu, choose Update Index/Table. Writer updates the table of contents to reflect the changes in the document.

You can also update the index from the Navigator by right-clicking on Indexes → Table of Contents1 and choosing Index → Update from the pop-up menu.

(b) To delete the table of contents from a document:

(i) Right-click anywhere in the TOC.

(ii) From the pop-up menu, choose Delete Index/Table. Writer deletes the table of contents.

19. (a) There are 8 fields and 6 records in the table Employee.

(b) (i) `SELECT E_name, Salary FROM Employee WHERE Salary> = 22000;`

(ii) `SELECT* FROM Employee WHERE Commission IS NULL;`

(iii) `SELECT *FROM Employee WHERE Profile="SALESMAN";`

20. (i) **Entity Integrity** It defines the primary key of a table. Entity integrity rule on a column does not allow duplicate and null values.

(ii) **Domain Integrity** It defines the type, range and format of data allowed in a column. Domain integrity states that all values in a column must be of same type.

(iii) **Referential Integrity** It defines the foreign key concepts. Referential integrity ensures that data in related tables remains accurate and consistent before and after changes.

(iv) **User Defined Integrity** If there are some business requirements which do not fit any above data integrity then user can create own integrity, which is called user defined integrity.

21. Sunil can do the following:

- He should adjust his chair to support his lower back and ensure his feet are flat on the floor.
- His monitor should be at eye level to prevent neck strain. Using an ergonomic keyboard and mouse that reduce wrist extension can help alleviate wrist pain.
- Additionally, placing a document holder next to the monitor can reduce repetitive head movements.
- Regular breaks to stretch, move around, and perform exercises targeting the back and wrists are also essential.

SQP Code : **PB-3/10** Series *i*-**Succeed 3-25/10** Roll No. | | | | | | | | |

Sample Question Paper 03

Information Technology 10th (Code 402)

General Instructions

Time : 2 Hrs.

Max. Marks : 50

1. Please read the instructions carefully.
2. This Question Paper consists of 21 questions in two sections: Section A & Section B.
3. Section A has Objective Type Questions whereas Section B contains Subjective Type Questions.
4. Out of the given (5 + 16 = 21) questions, a candidate has to answer (5 + 10 = 15) questions in the allotted (maximum) time of 2 hours.
5. All questions of a particular section must be attempted in the correct order.
6. **Section A** Objective Type Questions (24 Marks)
   (i) This section has 5 questions.
   (ii) Marks allotted are mentioned against each question/part.
   (iii) There is no negative marking.
   (iv) Do as per the instructions given.
7. **Section B** Subjective Type Questions (26 Marks)
   (i) This section has 16 questions.
   (ii) A candidate has to do 10 questions.
   (iii) Do as per the instructions given.
   (iv) Marks allotted are mentioned against each question/part.

Section A Objective Type Questions *(24 Marks)*

1. Answer any 4 out of the given 6 questions based on Employability Skills. $(4 \times 1 = 4)$

(i) In a professional setting, which communication channel is most appropriate for discussing complex or sensitive issues?
(a) Social media platforms
(b) Face-to-face meetings
(c) Text messages
(d) Voicemails

(ii) .... stress is a result of body's response to deal with a dangerous situation or escape from it.
(a) Internal (b) Environmental
(c) External (d) Survival

(iii) An operating system that manages a group of independent computers and makes them appear to be a single computer is known as a .... operating system.
(a) real-time (b) graphical
(c) distributed (d) multi-user

(iv) An entrepreneur must form contacts with the .... to analyse the market.
(a) Planning
(b) Competitors
(c) Neighbours
(d) None of the above

(v) How can green skills contribute to poverty reduction?
(a) By creating job opportunities in sustainable sectors
(b) By encouraging overconsumption of resources
(c) By promoting deforestation for economic growth
(d) By neglecting social and community development

(vi) .... plays a major role in reaction to stress.
(a) Personality (b) Positive attitude
(c) Behaviour (d) None of these

2. Answer any 5 out of the given 6 questions. (5 × 1 = 5)

(i) In the Mail Merge dialog box, you can select the .... option if you want to save the merged documents.
(a) File (b) Edit (c) View (d) Format

(ii) Prerna is a student of class X. Her teacher has asked her to create a document on 'Women Empowerment'. She has written the text and also added relevant images in her document using Writer. But she has realised that the paragraph will look better if the images are placed around the text. Name the feature of writer she can use to get the desired result.
(a) Placing image (b) Positioning image
(c) Wrap text (d) Closing text

(iii) The grey colour in the TOC reminds us that the text has been generated ....
(a) manually (b) automatically
(c) Both (a) and (b) (d) None of these

(iv) Prashant is a writer. He has just completed writing his book using Writer software. Now, he wants to add a page which will contain the title of each chapter and its respective page number. Suggest the feature that can be used to do this task.
(a) Mail merge (b) Templates
(c) Styles (d) Table of contents

(v) Which of the following can be used to access a style menu?
(a) F11 function key
(b) Sidebar Menu
(c) Formatting toolbar
(d) All of the above

(vi) Which of the following is not the correct file extension for an image file?
(a) GIF (b) JPEG
(c) Odt (d) PNG

3. Answer any 5 out of the given 6 questions. (5 × 1 = 5)

(i) Alpana has made four spreadsheets containing marks of 5 subjects of all the students of her class. She has to prepare a sheet that contains the total marks of all the students of her class. Name the option that can be used to perform this task.
(a) Subtotal (b) Average
(c) Goal Seek (d) Scenario

(ii) .... is used in between the cell reference in a formula.
(a) : (b) ,
(c) Both (a) and (b) (d) @

(iii) Internally for each recorded macro, some code is generated, which is stored inside ...... and ...... clause.
(a) Sub, End Sub
(b) Section, End Section
(c) Function, End Function
(d) None of the above

(iv) A __________ hyperlink stores the location with respect to the current location.
(a) relative (b) absolute
(c) mixed (d) All of these

(v) Reviewers and authors can add their .... to explain their changes in the cell of Spreadsheet.
(a) Comments (b) Hyperlink
(c) Worksheet (d) Macros

(vi) Priya, Ravi and Suresh are working in the accounts department of an advertising company. They handle different set of clients. Now, they are collaborating to create a spreadsheet for maintaining records of all their clients combined together. Which option should they use so that they all can work simultaneously in the sheet?

(a) Add document
(b) Share document
(c) Combine document
(d) None of the above

4. Answer any 5 out of the given 6 questions. (5 × 1 = 5)

(i) The default data type for a field is ....

(a) char (b) int
(c) text (d) None of these

(ii) Field is the individual sub component of one ....

(a) record (b) column
(c) data (d) None of these

(iii) Which of the following is not true about queries?

(a) It can be created using multiple tables
(b) Multiple queries can be created in a database
(c) A query can run multiple times
(d) A query once created cannot be edited

(iv) Key field is a unique identifier for each record. It is defined in the form of

(a) rows (b) columns
(c) tree (d) query

(v) Which of the following commands is not a Data manipulation language?

(a) Select (b) Insert
(c) Update (d) Alter

(vi) Duplication of data is known as ....

(a) data security (b) data incomplete
(c) data redundancy (d) None of these

5. Answer any 5 out of the given 6 questions. (5 × 1 = 5)

(i) Which of the following is not considered a best practice for ensuring safety at the workplace?

(a) Regularly conducting safety drills
(b) Providing employees with personal protective equipment (PPE)
(c) Encouraging employees to skip breaks to maintain productivity
(d) Implementing a comprehensive emergency response plan

(ii) What does the term "PPE" stand for in the context of Workplace safety?

(a) Personal Protective equipment
(b) Prevention of potential emergencies
(c) Protective product evaluation
(d) Primary prevention exercises

(iii) Which of the following is an example of a physical hazard at the workplace?

(a) Repetitive motion injuries
(b) Exposure to toxic chemicals
(c) Poor lighting in work areas
(d) Stress due to tight deadlines

(iv) What is the most effective way to prevent falls from height at the workplace?

(a) Posting warning signs around elevated areas
(b) Providing training on fall prevention techniques
(c) Using guardrails, safety nets, or personal fall arrest systems
(d) Ensuring employees wear hard hats

(v) Which of the following is a common strategy to manage stress at work?

(a) Increasing workload to keep employees busy
(b) Encouraging regular breaks and physical activity
(c) Reducing communication between team members
(d) Ignoring employee concerns about workload

(vi) What is the purpose of a safety guidelines checklist in the workplace?

(a) To ensure employees work faster
(b) To identify and mitigate potential hazards
(c) To reduce the need for employee training
(d) To decrease the overall costs of workplace operations

Section B Subjective Type Questions *(26 Marks)*

Answer any 3 out of the given 5 questions on Employability skills. $(3 \times 2 = 6)$

Answer each question in 20-30 words.

6. What are the skills necessary for independent working? List any six.
7. What are the benefits of acquiring green skills?
8. What are the responsibilities of an operating system with respect to file management?
9. What are the disadvantages of entrepreneurship?
10. What are prepositions?

Answer any 4 out of the given 6 questions in 20-30 words each. $(4 \times 2 = 8)$

11. What is clone formatting in Writer?
12. What is a macro?
13. What is the role of key fields in a database? Name the keys in a DBMS.
14. List some of the IT workplace hazards.
15. Define the following terms:
    (i) Active Cell (ii) Sheet Tab
16. How can you prepare for emergencies?

Answer any 3 out of the given 5 questions in 50-80 words each. $(3 \times 4 = 12)$

17. Ishita is a teacher. She had entered the marks of all the students and also calculated the total of the students. Now, she wants to sort the data so that she can find the names of the students according to their marks in descending order. Tell her the different steps to sort the data.
18. Write the steps for text fitting inside a shape in a word processor document. Also, describe its options.
19. Consider the following table : Employee Salary.

Table : EmployeeSalary

LastName	FirstName	Dept	PayrollNumber	Salary (₹)	JobTitle
Shen	James	Finance	A621	19500	Payroll Clerk
Gupta	Shruthi	Finance	M502	35000	Accountant
Bedi	Reeta	Human Resource	M421	18500	Secretary
Walker	Tia	Sales	W815	24000	Sales Representative
Shafia	Ahmed	Factory	H219	39000	Factory Manager
Mittal	Chavi	Purchasing	M134	20000	Purchasing Clerk

(i) How many fields and records are there in the table EmployeeSalary?

(ii) Write the SQL queries for the following:

(a) List all data of table EmployeeSalary.

(b) Display all the records whose salary is less than 25000.

(c) Display the FirstName and JobTitle of employees having Dept 'Finance'.

20. What do you mean by Data Control language? Also, give its types.
21. GreenTech Industries is a manufacturing company. Recently, there have been growing concerns from the employees and environmental groups about the impact of GreenTech's operations on the surrounding environment, specifically regarding air and water pollution. Complaints have been made about the quality of air due to emissions from the factory and the potential contamination of a nearby river from industrial waste.

    As an environmental consultant, you have been asked to draft a set of guidelines for GreenTech Industries to follow in order to keep the surrounding air and water clean. What guidelines would you recommend and why?

SP-03

Answers *in Topper's Style*

My Commitment *I affirm that I am reviewing these solutions only after I have solved the Sample Question Paper 3 on my own. My purpose of looking the solutions is solely to verify whether my answers/solutions were correct or not and to identify my mistakes in case my solutions were wrong or I could not solve that.*

1. (i) (b), (ii) (d), (iii) (c), (iv) (b), (v) (a), (vi) (c)

2. (i) (a), (ii) (c), (iii) (b), (iv) (d), (v) (d), (vi) (c)

3. (i) (a), (ii) (a), (iii) (a), (iv) (a), (v) (a), (vi) (b)

4. (i) (c), (ii) (a), (iii) (d), (iv) (b), (v) (d), (vi) (c)

5. (i) (c), (ii) (a), (iii) (c), (iv) (c), (v) (b), (vi) (b)

6. The skills necessary for independent working are:

(i) Becoming self-aware, self-monitoring and self-correcting.

(ii) Knowing what we need to do.

(iii) Taking the initiative rather than waiting to be told what to do.

(iv) Doing what is asked to the best of our ability, without the need for external prodding, and working until the job is completed.

(v) Taking ownership of our mistakes without looking for excuses.

(vi) Refusing to let self-doubt or negative emotions due to negative past experiences take us away from the task.

7. Acquiring green skills can lead to improved employability, career growth and job opportunities in emerging green sectors. It also contributes to a more sustainable and resilient society.

8. The operating system is responsible for the following activities in connection with file management :

- Allocating and deallocating memory space as needed.
- Creating and deleting files and directories to organise files.
- Supporting primitives for manipulating files and directories.
- Mapping files onto secondary storage.
- Backing up files on stable (non-volatile) storage media.

9. Some of the disadvantages of entrepreneurship are as follows :

1. **Huge time Commitment** Starting and running a business demands a significant amount of time and dedication. Success requires a substantial time commitment.
2. **Risk** Entrepreneurship involves a high risk of loss of the business fails, it can deplete personal savings and resources.
3. **Hard Work** Entrepreneurs need to put in a lot of work to ensure their business becomes successful. The efforts required can be immense.

10. It is a word placed before a noun or pronoun to link it to another word in the sentence. Example: The mouse jumped **off** the table **onto** the floor **of** the room.

11. In LibreOffice Writer, clone formatting is a handy tool that lets you copy the formatting of text from one part of your document and apply it to another. This formatting can include things like font style, size, color, and even paragraph settings. It's like using a paintbrush to copy and paste formatting instead of text itself.

12. A macro is a saved sequence of commands or keystrokes that are stored for later use. An example of a simple macro is one that "types" your address. The Libre Office macro language is very flexible, allowing automation of both simple and complex tasks. Macros are especially useful to repeat a task the same way over and over again.

13. The key is defined as the column or the set of columns of the database table which is used to identify each record uniquely in a relation. e.g. If a table has id, name and address as the column names then say id is the *key* for that table as it is a unique identifier for each record.

Alternate, foreign, primary and candidate are a few types of keys in a DBMS.

14. IT workplace hazards include repetitive strain injuries (RSIs), eye strain from prolonged screen time, exposure to electromagnetic fields (EMFs), poor ergonomics leading to musculoskeletal issues, and mental stress from high workloads or tight deadlines.

15. (i) **Active Cell** The cell with the black outline in a spreadsheet data is always entered into the active cell.

(ii) **Sheet Tab** The tab at the bottom of a worksheet display the names of the worksheets, such as Sheet 1, Sheet 2 etc. Switching between worksheets can be done by clicking on the tab of the Sheet which you want to access.

16. To prepare for emergencies, follow the given guidelines

(i) Follow workspace protocol and guidelines to ensure safety and health; know and understand rules and procedures concerning fire emergencies.

(ii) Ensure that smoke alarms and sprinkler systems are installed, working properly and are not blocked.

(iii) Conduct regular fire drills.

17. Ishita can highlight the cells to be sorted, then select Data → Sort to open the Sort dialog, or click the Sort Ascending or Sort Descending toolbar buttons. Using the dialog, you can sort the selected cells using up to three columns, in either ascending (A-Z, 1-9) or descending (Z-A, 9-1) order.

18. Assume you want to create some shapes which have text in them. Some of the text might wrap within the shape.To do this,you have to right-click and choose Text and go back to the Text Tab and check the option Word wrap Text in Shape. In this way,the text gets wrapped inside a shape.You can also resize the shape to fit text.

To format the text in a shape Select the object to which text was added. Select Format → Text or right-click on the shape and select Text from the pop-up menu. The Text dialog is displayed.

19. (i) There are 6 fields and 6 records in the table EmployeeSalary.

(ii) (a) `SELECT * FROM EmployeeSalary;`

(b) `SELECT * FROM EmployeeSalary WHERE Salary<25000;`

(c) `SELECT FirstName, JobTitle FROM EmployeeSalary WHERE Dept='Finance';`

20. Data Control Language (DCL) deals with the commands used in SQL that permits a user to access, modify or work on the different priviledges in order to control the database. It allows the database owner to give access, revoke access and change the given permissions as and when required. DCL is basically used for enforcing data security.

The DCL commands present in SQL are

(i) **GRANT** It is used to grant (given access to) security priviledges to specific database users. It is mostly used to INSERT, DELETE, SELECT, UPDATE, EXECUTE, ALTER or to provide priviledges to user's data.

Syntax GRANT <priviledges> ON <object name> To <user/roles>

(ii) **REVOKE** It is used to revoke with draw the permissions/access that was granted via GRANT command.

Syntax REVOKE <priviledges> ON <object name> FROM <user/roles>

21. A proper guideline may be followed by organisation to keep the surrounding air and water clean. Some of the points of such guidelines can be

1. Avoid dust production, generation of solid particles and gases in the air.
2. Organisation must use limited number of vehicles to avoid air pollution. Practice a no vehicle day in every week.
3. Ozone produced in the air can pollute the air. Many times, it is called as a smog. The generation of ozone gas must be kept at low level by the organisation.
4. Most of the human activities pollute the surrounding water. The sewage or the waste water can also cause the water pollution. Take care that their waste is not mixed with the surrounding water.

SQP Code : **PB-4/10** | Series ***i*-Succeed 4-25/10** | Roll No.

Sample Question Paper 04

Information Technology 10th (Code 402)

General Instructions

Time : 2 Hrs.

Max. Marks : 50

1. Please read the instructions carefully.
2. This Question Paper consists of 21 questions in two sections: Section A & Section B.
3. Section A has Objective Type Questions whereas Section B contains Subjective Type Questions.
4. Out of the given (5 + 16 = 21) questions, a candidate has to answer (5 + 10 = 15) questions in the allotted (maximum) time of 2 hours.
5. All questions of a particular section must be attempted in the correct order.
6. **Section A** Objective Type Questions (24 Marks)
   (i) This section has 5 questions.
   (ii) Marks allotted are mentioned against each question/part.
   (iii) There is no negative marking.
   (iv) Do as per the instructions given.
7. **Section B** Subjective Type Questions (26 Marks)
   (i) This section has 16 questions.
   (ii) A candidate has to do 10 questions.
   (iii) Do as per the instructions given.
   (iv) Marks allotted are mentioned against each question/part.

Section A Objective Type Questions *(24 Marks)*

1. Answer any 4 out of the given 6 questions based on Employability Skills (4 × 1 = 4)

(i) Managing stress is about making a plan to be able to cope effectively with daily pressures. Always keep in mind the ABC of stress management. The acronym ABC stands for
(a) Ability, Burden, Concise
(b) Adore, Belief, Cause
(c) Adversity, Beliefs, Consequences
(d) Adapt, Balance, Cooperate

(ii) The good stress is called........... .
(a) eustress (b) emstress
(c) Both (a) and (b) (d) None of these

(iii) Windows 10 is an operating system developed by ....
(a) Microsoft™ (b) IBM
(c) Samsung (d) Sony

(iv) How can an entrepreneur get the work done from his/her team?
(a) By creating a spirit of teamwork
(b) By motivation
(c) Using harsh words and actions
(d) Both (a) and (b)

(v) What is the importance of feedback in communication?
(a) It allows the speaker to dominate the conversation

(b) It helps in avoiding any further communication
(c) It facilitates understanding, clarification, and improvement
(d) It discourages active listening

(vi) What is the primary goal of green skills training?
(a) To reduce employment opportunities
(b) To promote sustainable practices and industries
(c) To prioritize economic growth over environmental concerns
(d) To discourage technological advancements

2. Answer any 5 out of the given 6 questions. (5 × 1 = 5)

(i) To start the macro recorder, which of the following command is used?
(a) Tools → Macros → Record Macro
(b) Tools → Record → Record Macro
(c) Data→ Macros → Record
(d) None of the above

(ii) In a document, you can insert ....
(a) Pictures
(b) ClipArts
(c) Shapes
(d) All of the above

(iii) Page styles affect a
(a) whole paragraph
(b) whole page
(c) group of characters
(d) group of items

(iv) If a table has to be created which tab and group should be used?
(a) Insert tab → Tables group
(b) Home tab → Tables group
(c) Design tab → Tables group → Table → insert Table
(d) None of the above

(v) In the hierarchy of headings, the lower - level headings pertain to .... and ....
(a) section, sub-sections
(b) headings, sub-headings
(c) Both (a) and (b)
(d) None of the above

(vi) To create the link from one document to another, both the documents should be
(a) open (b) closed
(c) Both (a) and (b) (d) None of these

3. Answer any 5 out of the given 6 questions. (5 × 1 = 5)

(i) Cell referencing can be done by using a .... as well as ....
(a) keyboard, windows menu
(b) keyboard, mouse
(c) windows menu, mouse
(d) None of the above

(ii) Full form of OLE is ....
(a) Object Linked and Embedded
(b) Option Linking and Embedding
(c) Open Linking and Embedding
(d) Object Linking and Embedding

(iii) We can rename a new sheet in Calc.
(a) After inserting a new sheet
(b) While inserting a new sheet
(c) Both (a) and (b)
(d) None of the above

(iv) In Calc, the comments are added
(a) automatically
(b) by author
(c) by reviewer
(d) Both (b) and (c)

(v) In order to group sheets, while holding the...... key, click on the Sheets tab you want to group.
(a) Alt (b) Shift
(c) Ctrl (d) Tab

(vi) In Calc, you can insert the data from different databases and other data sources. One such format is
(a) odd (b) .dbms
(c) .odb (d) .ods

4. Answer any 5 out of the given 6 questions. (5 × 1 = 5)

(i) After adding the data source, you need to specify the salutation. The selected salutation will be displayed in the pane.
(a) salutation (b) preview
(c) display (d) None of these

(ii) Which of the following is not the main building block of a database?
(a) Lists (b) Queries
(c) Reports (d) Forms

(iii) TCL commands are used to manage ...... in database.
(a) data (b) values
(c) transactions (d) None of these

(iv) ...... leads to data inconsistency.
(a) Data integrity (b) Data sharing
(c) Data redundancy (d) Data recovery

(v) .... is an inquiry into the database made using the SELECT statement.
(a) Query (b) Data
(c) Equation (d) None of these

(vi) Which of the following is a single piece of data?
(a) Field (b) Table
(c) Record (d) Form

5. Answer any 5 out of the given 6 questions. $(5 \times 1 = 5)$

(i) Every organisation must provide healthy and safety working environment for their employees at the ______.
(a) Home (b) Workplace
(c) Society (d) All of these

(ii) Every organisation must have separate ________ department.
(a) Security (b) Food
(c) Transportation (d) Psychological

(iii) The shape of warning sign is _____
(a) circular
(b) square
(c) triangular
(d) rectangular

(iv) Injuries and illness of the employees is prevented through national policy on __________.
(a) Occupational Safety
(b) Occupational Health
(c) Security
(d) Occupational Health and Safety

(v) Which of the following is not a situation when you do not need evacuation?
(a) Fire
(b) Earthquake
(c) Raining
(d) Hurricane

(vi) Ergonomics is the science concerned with _________ and arranging things.
(a) optimizing (b) designing
(c) modifying (d) improving

Section B Subjective Type Questions *(26 Marks)*

Answer any 3 out of the given 5 questions on Employability Skills. $(3 \times 2 = 6)$

Answer each question in 20-30 words.

6. What happens during meditation that makes it a useful technique for managing stress?

7. What strategies can a communication sender use to overcome information overload as a barrier?

8. Explain any two items of the Windows desktop.

9. Explain the role and significance of entrepreneurs.

10. Why are green skills important?

Answer any 4 out of the given 6 questions in 20-30 words each. $(4 \times 2 = 8)$

SP-04

11. What are objects in a word processing software?

12. Mention any two operations that can be performed using macros in a spreadsheet.

13. What is the use of AutoSum in spreadsheet?

14. A table named School (containing data of students of the entire school) is created, where each record consists of several fields including AdmissionNo (Admission Number), RollNo (Roll Number), Name. Which field out of these three should be set as the primary key and why?

15. What is an emergency action plan?

16. What type of keyboard is suitable to work on computer?

Answer any 3 out of the given 5 questions in 50-80 words each. (3 × 4 = 12)

17. Explain the Scenario tool of a spreadsheet software.

18. Ojas had prepared a Table of Contents of the project work he had done in a word processor application.

(a) Tell him the different steps to update the TOC

(b) Tell him the different steps to delete the TOC

19. Consider the following table: SummerCamp.

Table : SummerCamp

ChildID	FirstName	LastName	DOB	Gender	Group
109	Vedansh	Gupta	30/06/10	M	2A
214	Mack	Tyagi	09/12/08	M	1B
115	Aditi	Thakur	13/04/09	F	1A
108	Vikrant	Chauhan	02/02/09	M	2A
141	Swati	Saini	06/05/10	F	2B
233	Vishakha	Tyagi	01/08/10	F	3A
274	Madhur	Gupta	06/03/10	M	3B

(i) How many fields and records are there in the table SummerCamp?

(ii) Write SQL queries for the following:

(a) Display all the record of table SummerCamp whose DOB is between 02/02/09 and 06/03/10.

(b) Display all the records having Gender F.

(c) Display all the records according to the First Name.

20. Lavish wants to know the following points about database.

(a) Definition of a Database Management System.

(b) Any two advantages of using database management system for school.

21. Imagine you are the manager of a mid-sized manufacturing company. Recently, there have been several incidents at your workplace that have raised concerns about health, safety, and security. Reports are there that of workplace hazards affecting employee morale and productivity.

As the manager, find the key reasons for implementing Health, Safety, and Security Programs or Policies in the workplace.

Answers in Topper's Style

My Commitment *I affirm that I am reviewing these solutions only after I have solved the Sample Question Paper 4 on my own. My purpose of looking the solutions is solely to verify whether my answers/solutions were correct or not and to identify my mistakes in case my solutions were wrong or I could not solve that.*

1. (i) (c), (ii) (a), (iii) (a), (iv) (d), (v) (c), (vi) (b)
2. (i) (a), (ii) (d), (iii) (b), (iv) (a), (v) (c), (vi) (a)
3. (i) (b), (ii) (d), (iii) (c), (iv) (d), (v) (c), (vi) (c)
4. (i) (b), (ii) (a), (iii) (c), (iv) (c), (v) (a), (vi) (a)
5. (i) (b), (ii) (a), (iii) (c), (iv) (d), (v) (c), (vi) (b)
6. During meditation, we change from our normal activities to silence. We go beyond the noisy thoughts in the mind and enter a state of restful alertness, thus reducing stress. At this time, although we are in a state of deep rest, our mind is fully alert and awake. Thus, the body experiences many healing effects which are the reverse of the 'fight-or-flight' response, such as decreased heart rate, normalisation of blood pressure, deeper breathing, reduced production of stress hormones, higher immunity, more efficient use of oxygen by the body and reduced inflammation. All these changes in body function help in managing stress effectively.
7. To overcome the barrier of information overload, the sender of a communication must try to eliminate unnecessary information and stick to only important information in the communication.
8. Any two items of the Windows desktop are:

   Taskbar It is present in the bottom area of the desktop. It contains Start button, Cortana, Task View button, Quick Launch Bar and Notification Area.

   Icons The small pictures on the desktop which represent various programs/applications are called icons.
9. The role and significance of entrepreneurs are discussed below:
   (i) **Organiser of Society's Productive Resources**
   She/He assembles the unused natural, physical and human resources of the society, combines them properly, establishes effective coordination between them and makes the economic activities dynamic.
   (ii) **Helpful in Capital Formation** An entrepreneur is helpful in capital formation as we know that increase in the rate of capital formation is quite essential for the economic development of any country.
   (iii) **Increase in Employment Opportunities** An entrepreneur creates maximum employment opportunities in the society by way of establishing new industries, developing and expanding the existing industries and by undertaking innovative activities.
10. Green skills are important because they enable individuals to participate in the transition to a greener economy and address environmental challenges such as climate change, pollution, and resource depletion.
11. The word processor object allows different formatting within the same object. However, word processor objects are printed as an image, so they require quite a bit more resources than a normal single or multiline text objects. Word processing objects include text, graphical and embedded objects.
12. Macros can be used for the following operations:
    (i) If formatting settings need to be applied repeatedly in a spreadsheet then, macros can be used.
    (ii) Macros can be used to sort data and to apply mathematical functions or formulas.
13. When working with large spreadsheets containing a considerable number of rows or columns with data, it is often needed AutoSum with a quick click of a menu or button instead of manually typing the SUM function. LibreOffice spreadsheet program Calc has this feature.
    (i) Open any Calc workbook with numbers and data, or open your workbook.
    (ii) Select the cell where you would like to put the autosum of your data.
    (iii) Click on the sigma icon beside the formula bar and click Sum from the dropdown menu. You can see the Sum is calculated automatically.
14. AdmissionNo_should be set as the primary key because admission numbers are unique for each and every student of the school, which is not possible in the case of RollNo and Name.
15. An Emergency Action Plan (EAP) is a written document that outlines how to respond to various types of emergencies in a workplace or community space. It's a key part of an organization's safety procedures and can help reduce injuries, property damage, and ensure visitor safety.
16. The keyboard should tilt and separate from the screen to find a comfortable working position and avoid fatigue in the arms or hands. The space in front of the keyboard must be sufficient to provide support for the hands and arms of the user. The keyboard should have a matt surface to avoid reflective glare.

17. A Scenario is a set of values that Calc saves for a group of cells. Whenever we run a scenario Calc automatically substitutes the saved cell values into a connected formula to give us an output. By having different scenarios for a same group of cells we can get different results from the formula and compare these results to know which is the most suitable set of values for us. For example, if you wanted to calculate the effect of different interest rates on a car loan, you could add a scenario for each interest rate, and quickly view the results. This will help you to easily find out the most desirable rate of interest for availing the loan. Clearly, a Scenario is a tool to test "what-if" questions e.g., what happens if I replace THIS value by THAT value. Each scenario has a name, and can be edited and formatted separately. You can easily switch between different scenarios for a group of cells by using the scenario drop down list or scenario navigator.

18. (a) To update a table of contents when changes are made to the document:

(i) Right-click anywhere in the TOC.

(ii) From the pop-up menu, choose Update Index/Table. Writer updates the table of contents to reflect the changes in the document.

You can also update the index from the Navigator by right-clicking on Indexes → Table of Contents1 and choosing Index → Update from the pop-up menu.

(b) To delete the table of contents from a document:

(i) Right-click anywhere in the TOC.

(ii) From the pop-up menu, choose Delete Index/Table. Writer deletes the table of contents.

19. (i) There are 6 fields and 7 records in the table SummerCamp.

(ii) (a) `SELECT * FROM SummerCamp WHERE DOB BETWEEN 02/02/09 AND 06/03/10;`

(b) `SELECT * FROM SummerCamp WHERE Gender='F';`

(c) `SELECT * FROM SummerCamp ORDER BY FirstName;`

20. (a) Database Management System (DBMS) is a collection of programs that enable users to create, maintain database and control all the access to the database. The primary goal of the DBMS is to provide an environment that is both convenient and efficient for user to retrieve and store information.

(b) The advantages of using DBMS for school are as follows:

(i) In school, DBMS is used to store the data about students, teachers and any other related things at a centralised location.

(ii) It provides security to the personal information of the school, stored in it.

21. There are several reasons that can be specified for safety policy as given below.

- It clearly indicates the company's commitment for their employee's health and safety.
- It shows the performance of the business and the safety performance are compatible with each other.
- It clearly state that the company is not only doing the business for profits but it is taking care of all its stake holders.
- The accountability of every one working for the company is outlined for the workplace health, safety and security.
- Company can comply national policy on Occupational Health and Safety (OH&S) of Government of India.
- Injuries and illness of the employees is prevented through such policy.

SQP Code : **PB-5/10** Series ***i*-Succeed 5-25/10** Roll No.

Sample Question Paper 05

Information Technology 10th (Code 402)

General Instructions

Time : 2 Hrs.

Max. Marks : 50

1. Please read the instructions carefully.
2. This Question Paper consists of 21 questions in two sections: Section A & Section B.
3. Section A has Objective Type Questions whereas Section B contains Subjective Type Questions.
4. Out of the given (5 + 16 = 21) questions, a candidate has to answer (5 + 10 = 15) questions in the allotted (maximum) time of 2 hours.
5. All questions of a particular section must be attempted in the correct order.
6. **Section A** Objective Type Questions (24 Marks)
   (i) This section has 5 questions.
   (ii) Marks allotted are mentioned against each question/part.
   (iii) There is no negative marking.
   (iv) Do as per the instructions given.
7. **Section B** Subjective Type Questions (26 Marks)
   (i) This section has 16 questions.
   (ii) A candidate has to do 10 questions.
   (iii) Do as per the instructions given.
   (iv) Marks allotted are mentioned against each question/part.

Section A Objective Type Questions *(24 Marks)*

1. Answer any 4 out of the given 6 questions based on Employability Skills. (4 × 1 = 4)

(i) A .... is a collection of information saved as a unit.
(a) Folder (b) File
(c) Path (d) File extension

(ii) .... generates within the human regarding the unreasonable matters.
(a) Internal stress
(b) Survival stress
(c) Environmental stress
(d) None of the above

(iii) Which of the following is an example of a barrier to effective communication?
(a) Active listening
(b) Providing clear instructions
(c) Language barriers
(d) Using appropriate body language

(iv) An entrepreneur must establish good relations with .... and its functionaries.
(a) customer
(b) government
(c) Both (a) and (b)
(d) None of the above

(v) Which of the following is not an environmental benefit of green skills?

(a) Reduction in greenhouse gas emissions

(b) Preservation of biodiversity

(c) Increased use of non-renewable resources

(d) Conservation of natural habitats

(vi) Sonika gets up at 6 AM and goes for her hobby classes. Then, she comes back home and finishes her homework before going to school. She does all work by herself. No one tells her to do so. This is called ....

(a) self-awareness

(b) self-motivation

(c) self-regulation

(d) discipline

2. Answer any 5 out of the given 6 questions. $(5 \times 1 = 5)$

(i) The structure line displays the elements for entries in the level column. The .... button represents the page number.

(a) # (b) &

(c) % (d)@

(ii) To delete a template, ... on a template in the Templates window and select Delete.

(a) Confirmation dialog box open

(b) Double-click

(c) Left-click

(d) Right-click

(iii) Which extension is given to a document by default in LibreOffice writer?

(a) .odt (b) .com

(c) .docx (d) .odf

(iv) Under .... tab, Bullet and Numbering, Page style etc options are present.

(a) Tools (b) Format

(c) Window (d) Table

(v) Which tab of Writer contains the Mail Merge Wizard?

(a) View (b) Tools

(c) Edit (d) Format

(vi) What keyboard Shortcut can be used to quickly align text to the center in the LibreOffice writer?

(a) Ctrl + C (b) Ctrl + E

(c) Ctrl + A (d) Ctrl + D

3. Answer any 5 out of the given 6 questions. $(5 \times 1 = 5)$

(i) Default name of first scenario created in Sheetl of Calc is ....

(a) Sheet_1_Scenario

(b) Sheet_Scenario_1

(c) Sheetl_Scenario_1

(d) None of the above

(ii) Group by is used in ________ tool to apply summary functions on columns.

(a) Consolidate function

(b) Group and Outline

(c) What-if scenario

(d) Subtotal tool

(iii) In the Subtotal dialog box, the .... box is used to select the column on which you want to add the Subtotal to.

(a) group by (b) filter by

(c) consolidate by (d) update by

(iv) In Goal seek dialog box, the .... we enter the reference of the cell that contains the value to be changed.

(a) variable cell

(b) modifying cell

(c) changing cell

(d) replacing cell

(v) If you are continually working with the same range, then you may give a name to the range using .... option under Data Menu.

(a) Define data

(b) Define range

(c) Define reference

(d) Define address

(vi) The comments that are added while creating a scenario is displayed in the .... while using scenario.
(a) preview pane
(b) navigator box
(c) comment window
(d) None of the above

4. Answer any 5 out of the given 6 questions. $(5 \times 1 = 5)$

(i) ...... command is used to restore database to original since the last COMMIT.
(a) REVIEW
(b) SELECT
(c) ROLLBACK
(d) None of these

(ii) Which of the following fields will not make a suitable primary key?
(a) A customer's account number
(b) A date-field
(c) An auto number field
(d) A student's admission number

(iii) .... command is used to retrieve data from a database.
(a) SELECT (b) INSERT
(c) UPDATE (d) None of these

(iv) Commands are a set of instructions that is used to interact with .... database.
(a) SQL (b) Java
(c) Mac (d) DBMS

(v) ...... is a collection of related information.
(a) Base
(b) Database
(c) Web-based
(d) None of the above

(vi) Which of the following is also known as computer based record keeping system?
(a) Data Manipulation System
(b) Computer Data System
(c) Computerised Record Keeping System
(d) DBMS

5. Answer any 5 out of the given 6 questions. $(5 \times 1 = 5)$

(i) Which of the following is considered a major factor contributing to stress at work?
(a) Flexible working hours
(b) Supportive management
(c) Excessive workload
(d) Employee recognition programs

(ii) Which of the following is typically included in a workplace safety guidelines checklist?
(a) Daily team-building exercises
(b) Personal protective equipment (PPE) requirements
(c) Employee birthday celebrations
(d) Flexible lunch breaks

(iii) What can extensive use of automobile vehicles on a campus lead to?
(a) Improved employee punctuality
(b) Increased air pollution
(c) Enhanced campus security
(d) Better parking availability

(iv) What is a common cause of a stiff neck?
(a) Drinking too much water
(b) Poor posture
(c) Eating spicy food
(d) Wearing comfortable shoes

(v) While using a keyboard, your fingers should be above __________.
(a) Home position
(b) Rest position
(c) Base position
(d) Spacebar

(vi) In children prolonged use of computers or electronics in general, is a major contributing factor to __________.
(a) Enhanced stress
(b) Obesity
(c) Hypertension
(d) ADHD

Section B Subjective Type Questions *(26 Marks)*

Answer any 3 out of the given 5 questions on Employability Skills. (3 × 2 = 6)

Answer each question in 20-30 words.

6. How can we self-motivate ourselves for completing a task which appears to be too large or too complex to be done by us?

7. What role does non-verbal communication play in effective communication?

8. Write any two main advantages of an operating system.

9. Describe the following functions of an entrepreneur:
   (i) Innovation
   (ii) Risk-Taking

10. How can green skills be acquired?

Answer any 4 out of the given 6 questions in 20-30 words each. (4 × 2 = 8)

11. Write some features of spelling checker in OpenOffice Writer.

12. How to create the reference with the mouse in Calc?

13. What is data analysis in a spreadsheet software?

14. Explain the term relational database management system.

15. What is conventional requirement for the workstation?

16. How do you establish evacuation routes and exits?

Answer any 3 out of the given 5 questions in 50-80 words each. (3 × 4 = 12)

17. Simran wants to know about Subtotal. Answer the given questions for her.
   (i) What is SUBTOTAL() function?
   (ii) Names of any 5 functions with their function index number.

18. Ram wants to compress a picture. Write the steps through which he can do so.

19. Consider the following table: MASTER

Table : MASTER

SNo	Name	Age	Department	Salary
1	Shyam	21	Computer	12000
2	Shiv	25	Maths	15000
3	Rakesh	31	Hindi	14000
4	Sharmila	32	History	20000
5	Dushyant	25	Software	30000

   (i) How many fields and records are there in the table MASTER?
   (ii) Write the SQL queries to:
      (a) Display all the records according to Age.
      (b) Display Name and Department of the person having salary less than 20000.
      (c) Display the Name of the person having age less than 30.

20. Yuan is learning about database. But, he didn't understand the concept of field, records and table. Answer to him the following queries:
   (i) How are fields, record and a table related to each other? Explain with the help of an example.
   (ii) What are the main purposes of a database system?

21. Reema has been appointed as SME in an IT based company. Tell her the following:
   (i) What is workplace emergency?
   (ii) Name the workplace emergencies that may happen.

SP-05

Answers *in Topper's Style*

My Commitment *I affirm that I am reviewing these solutions only after I have solved the Sample Question Paper 5 on my own. My purpose of looking the solutions is solely to verify whether my answers/solutions were correct or not and to identify my mistakes in case my solutions were wrong or I could not solve that.*

1. (i) (b), (ii) (a), (iii) (c), (iv) (c), (v) (c), (vi) (b)
2. (i) (a), (ii) (d), (iii) (a), (iv) (b), (v) (b), (vi) (b)
3. (i) (c), (ii) (d), (iii) (a), (iv) (a), (v) (b), (vi) (a)
4. (i) (c), (ii) (b), (iii) (a), (iv) (a), (v) (b), (vi) (d)
5. (i) (c), (ii) (b), (iii) (b), (iv) (b), (v) (a), (vi) (b)
6. For completing a task which appears to be too large or too complex to be done by us, we can break down the job into several smaller and easier tasks, each of which can be accomplished in a set time period. This is possible only through self-motivating ourselves to find a workable solution to the task, as self-motivation is our ability to identify effective methods of thinking about something to taking action about it. Breaking down the job into smaller tasks comprises the thinking part, whereas accomplishing each small part of the task comprises the 'taking action' part.
7. Non-verbal communication, such as body language, facial expressions, and gestures, complements verbal communication and adds meaning to messages. It helps convey emotions, attitudes, and intentions.
8. The main advantages of an operating system include:
   (i) Allows multiple programs to run concurrently.
   (ii) Simplifies the programming of application software because the program does not have to manage the hardware. The operating system manages all hardware and the interaction of software. It also gives the program a high-level interface to the hardware and ways of interacting with other programs.
9. (i) **Innovation** It includes introducing new products, opening new markets, new sources of raw material and new organisation structure.
   (ii) **Risk-Taking** An entrepreneur has to take risk by choosing one among various alternatives.
10. Green skills can be acquired through formal education programs, vocational training, apprenticeships, and on-the-job experiences that focus on sustainable practices and environmental management.
11. You can right-click on a word with a wavy underline, to open a context menu. If you select from the suggested words on the menu, the selection will replace the misspelled word in your text.

    You can change the dictionary language (for example, to Spanish, French or German) on the Spelling dialog box.

    The Options dialog of the Spelling tool has a number of different options, such as whether to check uppercase words and words with numbers.
12. **Creating The Reference With The Mouse** Look at the example below which shows a Marks Detail sheet with a blank Marks column. On the Marks detail sheet, set up a place for all five subject marks, so we know where to put the cell reference. We want to place the reference for the checking marks in cell B3.

    To make the cell reference in cell B3, select the cell and follows these steps.

    1. Click on the = icon next to the formula bar. The icon changes and an equals sign appears in the formula bars.
    2. Now, click on the sheet tab for the sheet containing the cell to be referenced. In this case, that is the Marks Detail sheet.
    3. Click on cell F3 in the Detail sheet.
    4. Click the green checkmark in the formula bar to finish.
13. Data analysis is a process of inspecting, cleansing, transforming, and modeling data with the aim of deriving useful information from it, which can further be used in an organization's decision making process. Calc offers several tools for analyzing and manipulating spreadsheets including data consolidation, subtotals, scenarios, Goal seek and Solvers etc. All these tools are organized in two menus-Tools menu and data menu.
14. RDBMS (Relational Database Management System) is a type of DBMS that stores data in the form of relations (tables). Relational databases are powerful, so they require few assumptions about how data is related or how it will be extracted from the databases.

    An important feature of relational database system is that a single database can be spread across several tables. Oracle, DB2, SAP, Sybase, ASE, Informix, Access etc. are the examples of RDBMS.
15. The workstation should be designed to provide sufficient space for the user to change position and vary movements. The user should have enough desk space for the equipment they use.
16. Establish evacuation routes and exits by identifying clear, unobstructed paths, marking them with visible signs, ensuring they are well-lit, regularly

maintaining them, and conducting periodic training and drills for all occupants.

17. (i) The SUBTOTAL function is listed in the mathematical category of functions. It is used to calculate subtotals for a given range with the help of another function defined within it. The general syntax of the SUBTOTAL function is as follows:

SUBTOTAL (Function; Range)

Here, Function is the index number for one of the functions

(ii) Any 5 functions with their function index number are:

Function	Function index
Average ()	1
Count ()	2
Counta ()	3
Max ()	4
Min ()	5

18. To resize an image:

1. Click one time on the image to select it.
2. From the Menu bar select: Format → Position and Size.
3. Choose the Position & Size tab.
4. Insert the desired image size and click the OK button.

19. (i) There are 5 fields and 5 records in the table MASTER.

(ii) (a) `SELECT * FROM MASTER ORDER BY Age;`

(b) `SELECT Name, Department FROM MASTER WHERE Salary<20000;`

(c) `SELECT Name FROM MASTER WHERE Age <30;`

20. (i) Fields are a type of information. A record contains logically related fields.

A table contains logically related records.

For example

Table : Emp

EmpNo	Name	Salary
1	Shridhar	20,000
2	Raghav	40,000

In table Emp, EmpNo, Name and Salary are three different fields. 1, Shridhar, 20,000 represents one complete record.

(ii) The main purposes of a DBMS are

(a) Storage of information

(b) Retrieval of information quickly.

(c) Sorting, selecting data that satisfies certain and readable format.

(d) Produce the report in some standardised and readable format.

21. (i) A workplace emergency is an unforeseen situation that threatens your employees, customers, or the public; disrupts or shuts down the workplace operations; or causes physical or environmental damage.

(ii) Emergencies may be natural or manmade and include the following:

- Floods,
- Hurricanes,
- Tornadoes,
- Fires,
- Toxic gas releases,
- Chemical spills,
- Radiological accidents,
- Explosions,
- Civil disturbances, and
- Workplace violence resulting in bodily harm and trauma.

SQP Code : **PB-6/10**   Series *i*-**Succeed 6-25/10**   Roll No.

Sample Question Paper 06

Information Technology 10th (Code 402)

General Instructions

Time : 2 Hrs.

Max. Marks : 50

1. Please read the instructions carefully.
2. This Question Paper consists of 21 questions in two sections: Section A & Section B.
3. Section A has Objective Type Questions whereas Section B contains Subjective Type Questions.
4. Out of the given (5 + 16 = 21) questions, a candidate has to answer (5 + 10 = 15) questions in the allotted (maximum) time of 2 hours.
5. All questions of a particular section must be attempted in the correct order.
6. **Section A** Objective Type Questions (24 Marks)
   (i) This section has 5 questions.
   (ii) Marks allotted are mentioned against each question/part.
   (iii) There is no negative marking.
   (iv) Do as per the instructions given.
7. **Section B** Subjective Type Questions (26 Marks)
   (i) This section has 16 questions.
   (ii) A candidate has to do 10 questions.
   (iii) Do as per the instructions given.
   (iv) Marks allotted are mentioned against each question/part.

Section A Objective Type Questions *(24 Marks)*

1. Answer any 4 out of the given 6 questions based on Employability Skills. (4 × 1 = 4)

(i) Effective communication is important in the workplace because it
(a) Enhances personal relationships
(b) Improves productivity and efficiency
(c) Reduces conflict and misunderstandings
(d) All of the above

(ii) Which of the following is an example of green building design?
(a) Constructing buildings with no regard for energy efficiency
(b) Using renewable materials for construction
(c) Increasing waste generation during construction
(d) Ignoring water conservation measures

(iii) Stress management infuses a sense of .... and accomplishment.
(a) pressure (b) control
(c) threat (d) None of these

(iv) A .... is a network security device that monitors incoming and outgoing network. It restricts access to unwanted sites.
(a) firewall (b) anti-virus
(c) block sites (d) None of these

(v) .... are the people who are too focused on what others think and they fail to focus on their internal matters.
(a) Seekers (b) Introspectors
(c) Gold diggers (d) Pleasers

(vi) From the following statements, which one is not the positive impact of entrepreneurship on society?
(a) Stimulates Innovation and Efficiency
(b) Creates jobs and Employment Opportunities
(c) Solves the problems of the society
(d) Discourages welfare of the society

2. Answer any 5 out of the given 6 questions. (5 × 1 = 5)

(i) To avoid inconsistency in formatting and reduce time and effort in formatting a document, we use ____________ in Writer.
(a) Styles (b) Templates
(c) Macro (d) Clipart

(ii) If you choose styles, and then change the base style then all the .... styles will change as well.
(a) linked (b) edited
(c) copied (d) None of these

(iii) Which tab of writer contains the Hyperlink option?
(a) File (b) Format
(c) Insert (d) Tools

(iv) To insert a symbol like © (copyright), you need to click on the...........option of the Insert tab.
(a) Special Character (b) Character
(c) Equation (d) Header

(v) Which option should be used to type H_2O,to get 2 to its proper place?
(a) Bold (b) Superscript
(c) Underline (d) Subscript

(vi) Which of the following is not a style type in Writer?
(a) Frame style (b) Image style
(c) List style (d) Character style

3. Answer any 5 out of the given 6 questions (5 × 1 = 5)

(i) Group and Outline in Calc is used to create an outline of the selected data and can group rows and columns together so that one can __________ to hide it or __________ it using a single click on it.
(a) Increase, Decrease
(b) Expand, Collapse
(c) Increase, Expand
(d) Decrease, Collapse

(ii) Which of the following tab is used to run Macro?
(a) Tools (b) Home
(c) Insert (d) Review

(iii) If you see #### in place of data in a cell, it means you need to .... the cell width.
(a) increase (b) decrease
(c) Both (a) and (b) (d) None of these

(iv) When a user inserts a new worksheet in spreadsheet software, the new worksheet will be inserted ....
(a) at the end of sheet tab
(b) in the beginning of sheet tab
(c) next to active sheet
(d) None of these

(v) In the given formula, identify the type of reference and the cells that are passed as arguments.
= Average(A5, B5)
(a) Absolute reference; cells are-A5 and B5
(b) Relative reference; cells are-A5 and B5
(c) Relative reference; cells are-A5 to B5
(d) Absolute reference; cells are-A5 to B5

(vi) In order to use data from a worksheet, you need to use its........... name.
(a) alias
(b) representative
(c) qualified
(d) quantified

SP-06

4. Answer any 5 out of the given 6 questions. (5 × 1 = 5)

(i) The extension of Database file of Base is

(a) .mdb (b) .xls
(c) .odb (d) .bdb

(ii) In __________ data type there can be only two values- True or False.

(a) Date (b) Char
(c) Boolean (d) Logical

(iii) Which one of the following is an example of RDBMS ?

(a) MongoDB
(b) Windows registry
(c) Publisher
(d) Oracle

(iv) A primary key field cannot be null, which also means that it cannot be ....

(a) invalid (b) positive
(c) alphanumeric (d) empty

(v) Information is the processed form of ....

(a) words (b) data
(c) sentence (d) records

(vi) DBMS provides various key fields as

(a) primary key and candidate key
(b) alternate key and foreign key
(c) Both (a) and (b)
(d) None of the above

5. Answer any 5 out of the given 6 questions. (5 × 1 = 5)

(i) Extensive use of fertilizers and pesticide must be avoided as it can make the ground water _________.

(a) Polluted
(b) Safe to use
(c) Safe for drinking
(d) Rich in minerals

(ii) Applying this organisation can reduce the potential for accidents, injury to improve performance and productivity.

(a) Ergonomics
(b) Rehabilitation
(c) Welfare schemes
(d) Right lighting

(iii) ___________ bright light, glare and flickering images can cause. eye strain and visual fatigue.

(a) LED's
(b) Television's
(c) Computer's
(d) Car's

(iv) Keep your monitor between ________ inches away from your face.

(a) 18 to 24 (b) 15 to 18
(c) 16 to 18 (d) 24 to 28

(v) __________ lighting from computer screens can trick your brain and suppress its release of melatonin substance that assists your sleeping patterns.

(a) Portable
(b) Artificial
(c) Colourful
(d) Dim

(vi) The ________ must be stable and allow the user to move easily and find a comfortable position.

(a) work chair (b) work table
(c) sofas (d) tables

SP-06

Section B Subjective Type Questions (26 Marks)

Answer any 3 out of the given 5 questions on Employability skills. (3 × 2 = 6)

Answer each question in 20-30 words.

6. Define nature walk as stress management technique.

7. How can individuals contribute to the development of green skills?

8. Explain the use of Antivirus for the protection of the computer system.

9. Describe the role of entrepreneurs.

10. How can active listening improve communication skills?

Answer any 4 out of the given 6 questions in 20-30 words each. (4 × 2 = 8)

11. Mention the steps to be followed to choose a style for a Word document?

12. Write the steps to freeze the columns.

13. What do you mean by relative cell referencing?

14. Describe various transaction control commands of SQL.

15. Give some examples of ignition sources.

16. Define the following :

(i) Accident in workplace (ii) Hazard

Answer any 3 out of the given 5 questions in 50-80 words each. (3 × 4 = 12)

17. Tanisha had created a Table of Contents of the project done by her. Tell her the different steps to do the following:

(i) Editing a TOC (ii) Updating a TOC

18. Simran wants to add comments in a spreadsheet application. Tell her the different steps involved in adding and editing comments.

19. Consider the following table ITEMS :

TABLE: ITEMS

Code	IName	Qty	Price	Company	TCode
1001	DIGITAL PAD 121	120	11000	XENITA	T01
1006	LED SCREEN 40	70	38000	SANTORA	T02
1004	CAR GPS SYSTEM	50	2150	GEOKNOW	T01
1003	DIGITAL CAMERA 12X	160	8000	DIGICLICK	T02
1005	PEN DRIVE 32 GB	600	1200	STOREHOME	T03

(a) How many fields and records are there in the table ITEMS?

(b) Write the SQL queries to:

(i) Display the detail of all the items in ascending order of item names (i.e., IName)

(ii) Display IName and Price of all those items, whose price is in the range of 10000 and 22000.

(iii) Display all the information of the items having price less than 10000.

20. Nupur wants to know the differences between the following:

(a) Fields and tuples (b) Data and information

21. Anil is a software developer working in a corporate office. Anil has been experiencing discomfort and strain in his eyes and neck, and he wants to ensure his workstation setup complies with these norms.

Given the scenario, what are the specific norms Anil should follow to optimize his display screen setup, and how can he adjust his current workstation to meet these standards?

SP-06

Answers *in Topper's Style*

My Commitment *I affirm that I am reviewing these solutions only after I have solved the Sample Question Paper 6 on my own. My purpose of looking the solutions is solely to verify whether my answers/solutions were correct or not and to identify my mistakes in case my solutions were wrong or I could not solve that.*

1. (i) (d), (ii) (b), (iii) (b), (iv) (a), (v) (d), (vi) (d)
2. (i) (b), (ii) (a), (iii) (c), (iv) (a), (v) (d), (vi) (b)
3. (i) (b), (ii) (a), (iii) (a), (iv) (c), (v) (a), (vi) (c)
4. (i) (c), (ii) (c), (iii) (d), (iv) (d), (v) (b), (vi) (c)
5. (i) (a), (ii) (a), (iii) (c), (iv) (a), (v) (b), (vi) (a)
6. **Nature Walks** It means walking in the local park or similar such activity. These walks may be done more than once a day for short periods of time during which we indulge in 'thought-stopping', i.e. not to think about our day-to-day activities. Such an activity will help us to avoid 'burn out', promote adequate sleep, ease muscle tension and decrease mental worries.
7. Individuals can contribute to the development of green skills by seeking training and education opportunities, advocating for sustainable practices in their workplaces, and supporting policies that promote the transition to a greener economy.
8. Antivirus software is a set of programs that can prevent, detect, remove and search for different viruses or other malware software like worms, trojan, adware, etc. Basically, the computer devices use this software but, it also works on networks and IT systems. Furthermore, it is not sufficient to just install this software rather, we also have to update them from time to time.
9. The role of entrepreneur are:
    1. They contribute towards the development of society by reducing concentration of income and wealth.
    2. They promote capital formation by mobilising the idle savings of the citizens and country's export trade.
    3. Entrepreneurs provide large-scale employment to artisans, technically qualified persons and professionals and work in an environment of changing technology and try to maximise profits by innovations.
    4. They enable the people to avail better quality goods at lower prices, which results in the improvement of their standard of living.
10. Active listening involves fully concentrating on the speaker, understanding their message, and responding appropriately. It promotes understanding, reduces misunderstandings, and strengthens relationships.
11.
    - Change the formatting of the object (paragraph, frame, etc) to your liking.
    - Open the Styles and Formatting window. From the icons at the top of the window, choose the type of style to create (paragraph, character, and so on).
    - In the document, select the item to save as a style.
    - In the Styles and Formatting window, click the New Style from Selection icon.
    - In the Create Style dialog box, type a name for the new style. The list shows the names of existing custom styles of the selected type, if any. Click OK to save the new style.
12. **Freezing single rows or columns**
    - Click on the header for the row below where you want the freeze or for the column to the right of where you want the freeze.
    - Select Window → Freeze.
    - A dark line will appear to indicate, where the freeze is put.

    Freezing a row and a column
    - Click into the cell that is immediately below the row you want frozen and immediately to the right of the column you want frozen.
    - Select Window → Freeze.
    - You will see two lines appear on the screen, a horizontal line above this cell and a vertical line to the left of this cell. Now, as you scroll around the screen everything above and to the left of these lines will remain in view.
13. A relative cell reference describes how far away a cell or group of cells is from another cell in the same spreadsheet. When dealing with a spreadsheet formula, the relative cell reference is the default behavior of a formula. For example, to add cells A2 and B2 together you could use the formula "=SUM(A2+B2)" in cell C2. If you were to copy that formula into cell C3, it would be relative to C3 and become "=SUM(A3+B3)."
14. Various transaction control commands of SQL are as follows
    (i) **COMMIT** Used to save the work done.
    (ii) **SAVEPOINT** Used to identify a point in a transaction to which you can later rollback.
    (iii) **ROLLBACK** Used to restore database to original, since the last COMMIT.
    (iv) **SET TRANSACTION** It establishes properties for the current transactions.
15. Examples of ignition sources include:
    - Open flames such as gas ovens, lighters in smoking areas, and welding torches.

- Sparks from wood or metal saws and other types of equipment.
- Heat sources such as combustion engines, space heaters, ovens, and machines that produce heat during operation.
- Chemical ignition from chemicals that combust under normal working temperatures.

16. (i) A workplace accident, also commonly known as an occupational accident, is an unforeseen event in the workplace that results in an injury, or a casualty, to an employee. It's described as a discrete event that occurs in the normal course of business, and can include events that occur on the company's premises, or off it.

A workplace accident can result in physical or mental harm (or both), including any injury, disease, or even death.

(ii) A hazard is a dangerous phenomenon, substance, human activity or condition. It may cause loss of life, injury or other health impacts, property damage, loss of livelihoods and services, social and economic disruption, or environmental damage.

17. (i) **Editing a table of contents**

To edit an existing table of contents

- Right click anywhere in the TOC.
- From the pop-up menu, choose Edit Index/Table.

The Insert Index/Table dialog box will appear. You can edit and save the table.

(ii) **Updating a table of contents**

Writer does not update the table of contents automatically, so after any changes to the headings, you must update it manually. To update a table of contents when changes are made to the document.

- Right click anywhere in the Table of Content.
- From the pop-up menu, choose Update Index/Table.

Writer updates the table of contents to reflect the changes in the document.

18. **Adding Comments to Changes**

Calc automatically adds to any recorded change a comment describing what was changed (for example, Cell B4 changed from '9' to '4'). Reviewers and authors can add their comments to explain their changes.

To add a comment to a change

1. Make the change to the spreadsheet.
2. Select the cell with the change.
3. Choose Edit → Changes → Comments. A dialog box will appear. The automatically added comment provided by Calc appears in the title bar of this dialog box and cannot be edited.
4. Type your own comment and click OK.

Editing change comments

1. Select the cell with the comment that you want to edit.
2. Select Edit → Changes → Comments.
3. Click OK.

19. (a) There are 6 fields and 5 records in table ITEMS.

(b) (i) `SELECT * FROM ITEMS ORDER BY IName;`

(ii) `SELECT IName, Price FROM ITEMS WHERE Price BETWEEN 10000 AND 22000;`

(iii) `SELECT * FROM ITEMS WHERE Price < 10000;`

Common Mistake Some students got confused in ORDER BY clause and GROUP BY clause. Students used GROUP BY clause for ascending the item names instead of ORDER BY clause.

20. (a) (i) **Fields or Columns (Data item)** It is an area (within the record), reserved for a specific piece of data. It is the individual sub-component of one record. It contains set of characters. e.g. Customer number, customer name, street address, city, state, phone number, current address, date of birth, etc. Field in a table is also known as **column** or **attribute**.

(ii) **Records or Rows or Tuples** It is the collection of data items of all the fields (information) pertaining to one entity or a complete unit of information, i.e. a person, company, transition etc. Record of a table is also known as **row**, **entity** or **tuple**.

(b) (i) **Data** In computing, data is information that has been translated into a form that is efficient for movement or processing. Relative to today's computers and transmission media, data is information converted into binary digital form.

(ii) **Information** Information is a vital component of our everyday lives. It is the raw material that fuels our decision-making, enables us to learn and grow, and helps us to communicate with one another.

21. The display screen should:

- Display well-defined characters of adequate size and spacing
- Have a stable image
- Have easily adjustable brightness and contrast
- Tilt and swivel easily to suit the user
- Be free from glare and reflections
- Use a separate base for the screen or an adjustable table
- Use the modern LED monitors of legible size and with adequate spacing between the characters and lines.

SQP Code : **PB-7/10** Series ***i*-Succeed 7-25/10** Roll No. [ ]

Sample Question Paper 07

Information Technology 10th (Code 402)

General Instructions

Time : 2 Hrs.

Max. Marks : 50

1. Please read the instructions carefully.
2. This Question Paper consists of 21 questions in two sections: Section A & Section B.
3. Section A has Objective Type Questions whereas Section B contains Subjective Type Questions.
4. Out of the given (5 + 16 = 21) questions, a candidate has to answer (5 + 10 = 15) questions in the allotted (maximum) time of 2 hours.
5. All questions of a particular section must be attempted in the correct order.
6. **Section A** Objective Type Questions (24 Marks)
   (i) This section has 5 questions.
   (ii) Marks allotted are mentioned against each question/part.
   (iii) There is no negative marking.
   (iv) Do as per the instructions given.
7. **Section B** Subjective Type Questions (26 Marks)
   (i) This section has 16 questions.
   (ii) A candidate has to do 10 questions.
   (iii) Do as per the instructions given.
   (iv) Marks allotted are mentioned against each question/part.

Section A Objective Type Questions *(24 Marks)*

1. Answer any 4 out of the given 6 questions based on Employability Skills. (4 × 1 = 4)

(i) Which of the following is not a type of entrepreneurship activities?
(a) Social
(b) Agricultural
(c) Women
(d) Leader

(ii) Which of the following is not a symptom of stress?
(a) Irritability
(b) Insomnia
(c) Fatigue
(d) Fever

(iii) When you start a computer, the operating system gets loaded into the main memory from the hard disk. This is called ....
(a) uploading
(b) booting
(c) starting
(d) downloading

(iv) Which of the following is a barrier to effective communication?
(a) Use of jargon and technical terms
(b) Clear and concise messaging
(c) Active listening
(d) Mutual understanding

(v) What is the role of green skills in waste management?
(a) Encouraging unsustainable disposal methods
(b) Promoting recycling and composting practices
(c) Increasing landfills and waste accumulation
(d) Disregarding the concept of resource conservation

(vi) The drive within you that compels you to complete tasks is
(a) self-motivation (b) self-regulation
(c) self-awareness (d) self-sufficient

2. Answer any 5 out of the given 6 questions (5 × 1 = 5)

(i) By holding ________ key and clicking on various object and can be used as one entity.
(a) Ctrl (b) Alt
(c) Shift (d) Arrow

(ii) In the Load Style dialog box, option loads the blank and the character styles from the selected document into the current document.
(a) Page (b) Paragraph
(c) Overwrite (d) Text

(iii) Which shortcut key is used for automatic spell checking?
(a) Shift + Insert (b) Shift + F7
(c) Ctrl + Insert (d) Tab + Insert

(iv) By dragging any .... handle you can increase or decrease the .... of the image diagonally.
(a) corner, size (b) side, quality
(c) top, depth (d) corner, quality

(v) .... ensure that all the documents have a standard layout, look and feel.
(a) Graphics (b) Layout
(c) Properties (d) Templates

(vi) What can be created by Libre Office Writer?
(a) Magazines journals
(b) Invitation cards
(c) Applications
(d) All of the above

3. Answer any 5 out of the given 6 questions. (5 × 1 = 5)

(i) Solve option under Tools menu amounts to a more elaborate form of .... The difference is that the Solver deals with equations with multiple ....
(a) unknown variables, goals seek
(b) variables, equation
(c) goal seek, unknown variables
(d) subtotal, goal seek

(ii) ________ scenario is a set of values that can be used within the calculations in the spreadsheet.
(a) What-if (b) Subtotal
(c) Consolidate (d) Editing

(iii) .... function takes data from a series of worksheets or workbooks and summaries it into a single worksheet that you can update easily.
(a) Summation
(b) Data Consolidation
(c) Data Format
(d) Data Chart

(iv) Which tab is used to share the worksheet data?
(a) Home (b) Review
(c) Insert (d) Layout

(v) .... can deal with multiple variables as the goal seek is used to manipulate one variable cell.
(a) Solver (b) Goal Seek
(c) Scenario (d) what-if

(vi) Rajat has received a spreadsheet, which is reviewed by his subordinates Puneet, Kavya and Aman, who made some corrections in it. Before Rajat shared the spreadsheet with his subordinates, he has activated the track changes feature. Which of the following option he should use now to keep some of the changes made by them?
(a) Accept and reject changes
(b) Overwrite and keep changes
(c) Both (a) and (b)
(d) None of the above

4. Answer any 5 out of the given 6 questions. (5 × 1 = 5)

(i) Databases have the ability to

(a) store a large amount of data in a structured format, easy update, sort query, production of reports.

(b) spell check, perform calculations, library of mathematical functions, replication.

(c) rotate images, copy and paste, fill scale.

(d) None of the above

(ii) Which of the following is an attribute whose value is derived from the primary key of some other table?

(a) Primary key (b) Foreign key
(c) Alternate key (d) None of these

(iii) A tuple in RDBMS is referred to .... of a table.

(a) record (b) field
(c) table (d) key

(iv) A relational database is a collection of

(a) attributes (b) tables
(c) records (d) fields

(v) .... determines the range of field values.

(a) Field Name (b) Data Type
(c) Field Size (d) Description

(vi) Which of the following is/are TCL commands?

(a) COMMIT (b) SAVE POINT
(c) ROLL BACK (d) All of these

5. Answer any 5 out of the given 6 questions. (5 × 1 = 5)

(i) Do not use the elevator in times of fire in the building. Always use .... for such emergencies.

(a) office space (b) staircase
(c) washroom (d) None of these

(ii) Every organisation must provide healthy and safety working environment for their employees at the _________.

(a) Home (b) Workplace
(c) Workstation (d) Parking

(iii) The most common definition of hazard is _________ that is associated with something.

(a) 'a danger or risk'
(b) 'a danger or support'
(c) 'support or risk'
(d) 'trigger or risk'

(iv) 'Stress at workplace can cause hazard in today's organisation.' State whether this statement is

(a) True (b) False

(v) Which type of hazard can cause skin irritation, illness or breathing problems?

(a) Chemical hazard
(b) Biological hazard
(c) Slipping hazard
(d) None of the above

(vi) If you have unsafe and unhealthy workplace, there will be higher days lost and will have higher

(a) employee satisfaction
(b) productivity
(c) stress levels
(d) None of these

Section B Subjective Type Questions *(26 Marks)*

Answer any 3 out of the given 5 questions on Employability skills. (3 × 2 = 6)

Answer each question in 20-30 words.

6. How does feedback contribute to improving communication skills?

7. What do you mean by environmental stress?

8. Explain the use of Disk Defragmenter.

9. Name two basic elements of entrepreneurship.

10. How can governments promote the development of green skills?

Answer any 4 out of the given 6 questions in 20-30 words each. (4 × 2 = 8)

11. How to add a comment in a word processor application?

12. Write the steps to sort the data in a worksheet.

13. What do you mean by Open Office Calc.

14. Mention any two components of a database.

15. Write a brief account of Occupational Overuse Syndrome.

16. What might be the cause of leg strain at workplace? How can we address it?

Answer any 3 out of the given 5 questions in 50-80 words each. (3 × 4 = 12)

17. What do you understand by text wrapping? Describe the various text wrapping tools and their uses.

18. Simran wants to add macro in a spreadsheet application. Tell her the different steps involved in adding a macro.

19. Consider the following table ITEM:

S_No	P_Name	S_Name	Qty	Cost	City
S1	Biscuit	Priyagold	120	12.00	Delhi
S2	Bread	Britannia	200	25.00	Mumbai
S3	Chocolate	Cadbury	350	40.00	Mumbai
S4	Sauce	Kissan	400	45.00	Chennai

(i) How many records and fields in the table ITEM?

(ii) Write the SQL queries to

(a) Display all the products whose quantity in between 100 and 350.

(b) Display the data for all products sorted by their quantity.

(c) To list S_Name, P_Name, Cost for all the products whose quantity is less than 400.

20. Answer the following questions regarding database:

(i) Mention any two databases.

(ii) Define different forms of a database.

(iii) What is an attribute whose value is derived from the primary key of some other table?

(iv) Define the SELECT command.

21. You are the safety manager at a large manufacturing plant that produces automotive parts. The plant operates 24/7 and employs over 500 workers. Recently, there have been several near-miss incidents and minor accidents on the factory floor. These incidents include slips, trips, falls, and minor injuries from machinery. Although no major injuries have occurred yet, the frequency of these incidents is increasing, causing concern among employees and management.

What steps would you take to assess the current safety situation and implement measures to prevent accidents and emergencies at the plant?

Answers in Topper's Style

My Commitment *I affirm that I am reviewing these solutions only after I have solved the Sample Question Paper 7 on my own. My purpose of looking the solutions is solely to verify whether my answers/solutions were correct or not and to identify my mistakes in case my solutions were wrong or I could not solve that.*

1. (i) (d), (ii) (d), (iii) (b), (iv) (a), (v) (b), (vi) (a)
2. (i) (a), (ii) (c), (iii) (b), (iv) (a), (v) (d), (vi) (d)
3. (i) (c), (ii) (a), (iii) (b), (iv) (b), (v) (a), (vi) (a)
4. (i) (a), (ii) (b), (iii) (a), (iv) (b), (v) (c), (vi) (d)
5. (i) (b), (ii) (b), (iii) (a), (iv) (a), (v) (a), (vi) (c)
6. Feedback provides valuable insights into one's communication strengths and areas for improvement. It helps individuals refine their approach, identify weaknesses, and adapt their communication style.
7. It is a response to happenings around us that cause stress, such as noise, pollution, crowding, pressure of work, family tensions etc. Some of these may be under our control if we try to control them, whereas some may not be controllable by us. Identifying these environmental stresses and learning to avoid them or deal with them will help lower our stress level.
8. Defragmentation is the process of consolidating fragmented files on the user's hard drive. Files become fragmented when data is written to disk, and there is not enough contiguous space to hold the complete file. Storage algorithms break the data apart so that it will fit into the available space.

   The process of defragmentation moves the data blocks on the hard drive around to bring all the parts of a file together. Defragmentation reduces file system fragmentation, increasing the efficiency of data retrieval and thereby improving the overall performance of the computer.
9. **Risk-Taking** Entrepreneurship and risk-taking go hand in hand. One of the most important features of entrepreneurship is that the whole business is run and managed by one person. So, there is no one to share the risks with.

   Vision Vision or foresight is one of the main driving forces behind any entrepreneur. It is the energy that drives the business forward by using the foresight of the entrepreneur. It is what gives the business an outline for the future – the tasks to complete, the risks to take, the culture to establish, etc.
10. Governments can promote the development of green skills by investing in education and training programs, creating policies that support sustainable industries, and providing incentives for businesses to adopt green practices.
11. To add a comment
    - Select the cell that the comment applies to.
    - Select Insert → Comment or right-click and select Insert Comment. The box shown in the figure below appears.
    - Type the text of your comment in the box.
    - Click outside the box to close it.

    Now the cell to which you added the comment has a colored dot in the upper right-hand corner. It does not have a colored border, unless the cell was also changed.
12. Sorting arranges the visible cells on the sheet. In Calc, you can sort by up to three criteria, with each criterion applied one after the other. Sorts are handy when you are searching for a particular item, and become even more powerful after you have filtered data.

    In addition, sorting is often useful when you add new information. When a list is long, it is usually easier to add new information at the bottom of the sheet, rather than adding rows in the proper places. After you have added information, you can then sort it to update the sheet.

    Highlight the cells to be sorted, then select Data → Sort to open the Sort dialog, or click the Sort Ascending or Sort Descending toolbar buttons. Using the dialog, you can sort the selected cells using up to three columns, in either ascending (A-Z, 1-9) or descending (Z-A, 9-1) order.
13. Calc is an easy to understand spreadsheet program that appeals to novice users and professional data miners and number crunchers alike.

    Calc provides a number of features not present in Excel, including a system which automatically defines a series for graphing based on the layout of the users's data. Calc is also capable of writing spreadsheets directly as PDF files.

    Calc can store a maximum of 65,536 rows with 1024 columns in each sheet with a maximum of 256 sheets.
14. Two components of database are as follows:

    Data It is raw numbers, characters or facts represented by value. Most of the organisations generate, store and process large amount of data. The data acts as a bridge between the hardware and the software. Data may be of different types such as User data, Metadata and Application Metadata.

Software It is a set of programs that lies between the stored data and the users of database. It is used to control and manage the overall computerised database. It uses different types of software such as MySQL, Oracle etc.

15. Occupational overuse syndrome, also known as repetition strain injury (RSI), is a collective term for a range of conditions, characterised by discomfort or persistent pain in muscles, tendons and other soft tissues, with or without physical manifestations. It is usually caused or aggravated by work, and is associated with repetitive movement, sustained or constrained postures and/or forceful movements.

16. Sitting to work for long time may cause strain in legs. Position your desk chair to sit comfortably with your feet flat on the floor and your lower legs vertical. Use a footrest for more support. Make sure that there's enough space to change position and stretch your legs out every now and then, too.

17. It allows the placement of image in relation to text. Text Wrapping tools are available under Drawing Object Properties Toolbar

Tool	Wrapping Effect
Wrap off	Text is placed above and below the image
Page Wrap	Text flows around the image. Moving an image will rearrange the text on the page
Optimal Page Wrap	In Page Wrap, if the space between image and margin is less than 2 cm then text will not be placed on that side
Wrap left	Text is placed on left side of the image
Wrap right	Text is placed on the right side of the image
Wrap through	Superimposes the image on the text

18. The following steps create a macro that performs paste special with multiply.

1. Open a new spreadsheet.
2. Enter numbers into a sheet.
3. Select cell A3, which contains the number 3, and copy the value to the clipboard.
4. Select the range A1:C3.
5. Use Tools → Macros → Record Macro to start the macro recorder. The Record Macro dialog is displayed with a Stop Recording button.
6. Use Edit → Paste Special. It will display the Paste Special dialog box.
7. Set the operation to Multiply and click OK. The cells are now multiplied by 3.
8. Click Stop Recording. The OpenOffice.org Basic Macros dialog box will appear.
9. Select the current worksheet. Existing worksheets show a library named Standard.

19. (i) There are 4 records and 6 fields.

(ii) (a) `SELECT * FROM ITEM WHERE Qty BETWEEN 100 AND 350;`

(b) `SELECT * FROM ITEM ORDER BY Qty;`

(c) `SELECT S_Name, P_Name, Cost FROM ITEM WHERE Qty < 400;`

Common Mistake Some students consider record as number of columns and field as number of rows. While records are number of rows and fields are number of columns present in a table.

20. (i) ORACLE, MySQL

(ii) There are four kinds of this database: document databases, key-value stores, column-oriented databases, and graph databases.

(iii) Foreign key

(iv) The SELECT command is used to select data from a database. The data returned is stored in a result table, called the result-set.

21. The steps that need to be taken are the following:

- Review incident reports and analyze patterns.
- Conduct safety audits to identify hazards.
- Gather employee feedback on safety concerns.
- Assess and prioritize risks based on likelihood and severity.
- Update safety policies to address risks.
- Develop SOPs for safe machinery operation and material handling.
- Establish an emergency response plan.
- Implement mandatory safety training for all employees.
- Conduct regular emergency drills.
- Install safety guards on machinery.
- Improve floor safety with non-slip coatings and clear signage.
- Ensure proper use of PPE by all employees.
- Conduct regular safety inspections.
- Implement an incident reporting system.
- Ensure active participation from top management in safety initiatives.
- Allocate resources for safety measures.

SQP Code : **PB-8/10** Series *i*-**Succeed 8-25/10** Roll No.

Sample Question Paper 08

Information Technology 10th (Code 402)

General Instructions

Time : 2 Hrs.

Max. Marks : 50

1. Please read the instructions carefully.
2. This Question Paper consists of 21 questions in two sections: Section A & Section B.
3. Section A has Objective Type Questions whereas Section B contains Subjective Type Questions.
4. Out of the given (5 + 16 = 21) questions, a candidate has to answer (5 + 10 = 15) questions in the allotted (maximum) time of 2 hours.
5. All questions of a particular section must be attempted in the correct order.
6. **Section A** Objective Type Questions (24 Marks)
   (i) This section has 5 questions.
   (ii) Marks allotted are mentioned against each question/part.
   (iii) There is no negative marking.
   (iv) Do as per the instructions given.
7. **Section B** Subjective Type Questions (26 Marks)
   (i) This section has 16 questions.
   (ii) A candidate has to do 10 questions.
   (iii) Do as per the instructions given.
   (iv) Marks allotted are mentioned against each question/part.

Section A Objective Type Questions *(24 Marks)*

1. Answer any 4 out of the given 6 questions based on Employability Skills. $(4 \times 1 = 4)$

(i) Which of the following best describes a "green skill job"?
(a) A job that focuses on recycling materials.
(b) A job that reduces the environmental impact of enterprises and economic sectors.
(c) A job that involves planting trees and conserving forests.
(d) A job that manages waste in urban areas.

(ii) Regular exercise helps pep up your mood and can take your mind off a lot of worry and negativity which are the main feed of stress. Which of the following activity is not considered as exercise?
(a) Walking (b) Jogging
(c) Swimming (d) Talking

(iii) Moving a folder or a file means .... it from its original location and placing it at another location.
(a) Removing (b) Leaving
(c) Pointing (d) None of these

(iv) Society plays a role in boosting entrepreneurship by
(a) creates needs and demands
(b) provides raw materials
(c) creates a need for education
(d) All of the above

(v) What is visual communication dependent on among people?
(a) Signs, symbols, and pictures
(b) Text messages
(c) Posture
(d) Body language

(vi) Which of the following is a social benefit of sustainable development?
(a) Increased income inequality
(b) Improved access to education and healthcare
(c) Limited job opportunities
(d) Neglected social infrastructure

2. Answer any 5 out of the given 6 questions. (5 × 1 = 5)

(i) .... styles are used to format graphics and text frames, including text wrap, borders, backgrounds and columns.
(a) Border (b) Frame
(c) Table (d) Text

(ii) ....is a list, usually found on a page before the start of a written work, of its chapter or section titles or brief descriptions with their commencing page numbers.
(a) Preface
(b) Table of contents
(c) Acknowledgements
(d) Page title

(iii) To add a new image to the Gallery, you can click on the .... button.
(a) New image (b) Add image
(c) New theme (d) Add theme

(iv) The .... alignment makes sure that none of the edges of text appear ragged.
(a) left (b) right
(c) center (d) justify

(v) .... controls how graphics are stacked upon each other or relative to the text.
(a) Arrangement (b) Alignment
(c) Anchoring (d) Wrapping

(vi) A ....can also be a quick way to take a list of people's mailing addresses and generate labels or envelopes with the address for a different person on each label or envelope.
(a) data source (b) database
(c) mail merge (d) E-mail

3. Answer any 5 out of the given 6 questions. (5 × 1 = 5)

(i) Neeta is planning to take a car loan to buy a new car. But she is not sure about the payback time, i.e. whether to pay it back in 5 or 6 years considering that her monthly fuel cost will also increase. In such cases, which of the following features of spreadsheet can she use to get an idea about it?
(a) Consolidation (b) Macros
(c) Templates (d) What-if analysis

(ii) This is a type of hyperlink available in Hyperlink dialog box, which creates a new worksheet.
(a) New document (b) New file
(c) New worksheet (d) New data

(iii) For sorting through macro, the selected cell range must be ....
(a) identical (b) different
(c) Both (a) and (b) (d) formatted

(iv) A worksheet is a
(a) collection of workbooks
(b) processing software
(c) combination of rows and columns
(d) None of the above

(v) .... function takes data from a series of worksheets or workbooks and summaries it into a single worksheet that you can update easily.
(a) Summation
(b) Data Consolidation
(c) Data Format
(d) Data Chart

(vi) Scenarios are tool test for .... questions.
(a) Auto
(b) Goal Seek
(c) What-if
(d) Drop Down

4. Answer any 5 out of the given 6 questions. (5 × 1 = 5)

(i) The .... command is used to modify the existing rows in a table.
(a) UPDATE (b) ALTER
(c) INSERT (d) REVIEW

(ii) A.............is a database element that is used to view, enter and edit records in a table.
(a) Form (b) Report
(c) Query (d) None of these

(iii) A .... language is a portion of a DML involving information retrieval only.
(a) DCL (b) Query
(c) TCL (d) None of these

(iv) The processed form of data is known as ....
(a) value (b) information
(c) knowledge (d) None of these

(v) State whether True or False.
Duplicate values can be entered in column marked as primary key.
(a) True (b) False

(vi) The candidate key, which is not used as primary key is called .... key.
(a) primary (b) foreign
(c) alternate (d) super

5. Answer any 5 out of the given 6 questions. (5 × 1 = 5)

(i) Which of the following is a fundamental safety rule to follow in the workplace?
(a) Always keep emergency exits locked.
(b) Wear appropriate personal protective equipment (PPE).
(c) Ignore safety signs and signals.
(d) Only report major injuries or accidents.

(ii) What is the most appropriate action to take if you discover a small fire in the workplace?
(a) Ignore the fire and hope it extinguishes itself.
(b) Evacuate the building immediately without warning others.
(c) Use a fire extinguisher to try and put out the fire if it is safe to do so.
(d) Pour water on the fire regardless of the type of fire.

(iii) What is one of the most effective ways to prevent slips, trips, and falls in the workplace?
(a) Use dim lighting to save energy.
(b) Keep walkways clear of obstacles and spills.
(c) Walk quickly to avoid spending too much time in risky areas.
(d) Wear shoes with slippery soles.

(iv) In the event of a workplace emergency, what is the first action you should take?
(a) Finish your current task before responding.
(b) Ignore alarms and continue working.
(c) Follow the emergency evacuation plan immediately.
(d) Call a friend to inform them of the situation.

(v) If an accident occurs and someone is injured, what is the first step you should take?
(a) Move the injured person to a different location.
(b) Leave the injured person and seek help from a supervisor.
(c) Assess the situation and call for medical assistance if needed.
(d) Ignore the injured person and continue working.

(vi) Which of the following practices is essential for maintaining a healthy lifestyle while working?
(a) Skipping meals to save time.
(b) Staying hydrated and taking regular breaks.
(c) Sitting for long hours without stretching.
(d) Avoiding all forms of physical exercise.

Section B Subjective Type Questions *(26 Marks)*

Answer any 3 out of the given 5 questions on Employability Skills. $(3 \times 2 = 6)$

Answer each question in 20-30 words.

6. What is the role of green skills in mitigating climate change?
7. Explain the term self-motivation.
8. Define multi-processing and multi-user operating system.
9. What do you mean by the term entrepreneur?
10. How can communication skills impact career success?

Answer any 4 out of the given 6 questions in 20-30 words each. $(4 \times 2 = 8)$

11. Describe the significance of using templates in your documents.
12. State the use of Consolidating Data in a spreadsheet.
13. What is cell reference? Also, write the use a cell reference in one or several formula.
14. Explain the term table used in database.
15. What are the essential steps to take when providing first aid for a minor burn?
16. What are the steps to apply first aid roller bandage to a wound?

Answer any 3 out of the given 5 questions in 50-80 words each. $(3 \times 4 = 12)$

17. Harmanpreet had inserted an image in a word processor application. Now, she wants to know the use of the following terms. Tell her the correct answer.
    (i) Alignment
    (ii) Anchoring
18. Samiksha wants to know the use of the following terms. Describe them for her.
    (i) Scenario (ii) Goal Seek
    (iii) Solver (iv) Subtotal
19. Consider the following

TABLE: APPLICANTS

No.	NAME	FEE	GENDER	C_ID	JOINYEAR
1012	Amandeep	30000	M	A01	2012
1102	Avisha	25000	F	A02	2009
1103	Ekant	30000	M	A02	2011
1049	Arun	30000	M	A03	2009
1025	Amber	40000	M	A02	2011

(i) How many records and fields are there in the table APPLICANTS.

(ii) Write the SQL queries to:

(a) Display NAME, FEE, GENDER, JOINYEAR about the APPLICANTS, who have joined before 2010.

(b) Display the NAMES of all APPLICANTS in ascending order of their JOINYEAR.

(c) Display the details of APPLICANTS of female.

20. Prashant wants to know about Data Manipulation language commands. Solve the following queries for him.
    (i) What is DML?
    (ii) Explain any three DML commands.
21. At a chemical manufacturing plant, workers handle hazardous substances daily. Recently, an employee suffered chemical burns due to improper handling of corrosive materials. This incident highlighted gaps in safety protocols and the need for enhanced protective measures.

    What steps should the plant management take to prevent similar incidents in the future?

Answers *in Topper's Style*

My Commitment *I affirm that I am reviewing these solutions only after I have solved the Sample Question Paper 8 on my own. My purpose of looking the solutions is solely to verify whether my answers/solutions were correct or not and to identify my mistakes in case my solutions were wrong or I could not solve that.*

1. (i) (b), (ii) (d), (iii) (a), (iv) (d), (v) (a), (vi) (b)
2. (i) (b), (ii) (b), (iii) (b), (iv) (d), (v) (a), (vi) (c)
3. (i) (d), (ii) (c), (iii) (c), (iv) (c), (v) (b), (vi) (c)
4. (i) (a), (ii) (a), (iii) (b), (iv) (b), (v) (b), (vi) (c)
5. (i) (b), (ii) (c), (iii) (b), (iv) (c), (v) (c), (vi) (b)
6. Green skills play a crucial role in mitigating climate change by facilitating the adoption of renewable energy, implementing energy-efficient technologies, and promoting sustainable practices that reduce greenhouse gas emissions.
7. Self-motivation refers to your ability to identify effective methods of making yourself move from thinking about something to taking action about it. Everyone is different.

   Some individuals are highly self-motivated, while others require external deadlines or some type of reward or penalty in order to move from thought to action. Identifying your specific needs in this area is the first step.
8. **Multi-Processing Operating System**
   - Use of two or more CPUs within a single computer system.
   - Simultaneous processing of two or more programs by multiple processors.
     e.g. Linux, Unix, Windows 2000, etc.

   Multi-User Operating System
   - It allows many users to take advantage of the computer's resources simultaneously.
   - It ensures that problem with one user doesn't affect the entire community of users.
     e.g. Unix, VMS, Linux, Windows 2000, etc.
9. An entrepreneur is someone who starts or owns a business. Whether it's in farming, retail, manufacturing or in the service sector, entrepreneurs are business people who find their success by taking risks. In their pursuits, they often become disruptors in established industries.
10. Strong communication skills are highly valued by employers as they contribute to effective teamwork, leadership, conflict resolution, and client relationships, all of which are crucial for career advancement.
11. 1. On using the standard templates, it is easy to create colour, attractive designs for slides.
    2. Easily one can modify the templates, even we can download from the Internet.
    3. Attractive designs of templates are available; it will be the audience to look up of the presentation.
    4. It creates attentive of audience.
    5. Quick customization of templates, text, fonts, pictures were available. –
    6. It has professional computer design.
12. Data Consolidation allows you to gather together your data from separate worksheets into a master worksheet. In other words, the Data Consolidation function takes data from a series of worksheets or workbooks and summaries it into a single worksheet that you can update easily.
13. A cell reference refers to a cell or a range of cells on a worksheet and can be used to find the values or data that you want formula to calculate.
    In one or several formulas, you can use a cell reference to refer to:
    - Data from one or more contiguous cells on the worksheet.
    - Data contained in different areas of a worksheet.
    - Data on other worksheets in the same workbook.
14. It is the building block of any relational database model, where all the actual data is defined and entered. A database consists of many tables. Tables (relations) consist of cells at the intersection of records (rows) and fields (columns). Different types of operations are done on the tables such as sorting, filtering, retrieving and editing of data. It is also known as a **file**.
15. For a minor burn, first cool the burn under running water for at least 10 minutes. Cover the burn with a sterile, non-adhesive bandage or clean cloth. Avoid applying creams or ointments. Seek medical advice if necessary.
16. To apply a roller bandage:
    - Keep the rolled part of the bandage above the injury and the unrolled part below the injury.
    - Begin by wrapping twice around the injury to hold the end in place.
    - Work up the limb, winding the bandage in spiraling turns, making sure that each new layer covers half of the previous one.
    - Finish by wrapping the bandage around once more and securing the end.

17. (i) Text alignment is a paragraph formatting attribute that determines the appearance of the text in a whole paragraph. For example, in a paragraph that is left-aligned (the most common alignment), text is aligned with the left margin. In a paragraph that is justified, text is aligned with both margins.

(ii) In programs like MS word or LibreOffice Writer, anchoring is used to keep objects like images or tables in a fixed position relative to the text. This ensures they don't jump around if you edit the surrounding content.

18. (i) **Scenarios** Scenarios are a tool to test "What-if" questions. Each scenario is named and can be edited and formatted separately. It is essentially a saved set of values for calculations. We can easily switch between these sets using the Navigator or a Drop-down list which can be shown beside the changing cells.

(ii) **Goal Seek** It is used to calculate a result based upon existing values. Using Goal Seek option under Tools menu, we can discover what values will produce the result that we want.

(iii) **Solver** It is an elaborated form of Goal seek. The difference is that the solver deals with equations with multiple unknown variables. It is specifically designed to minimize or maximize the result according to a set of rules defined by us.

(iv) **Subtotal** It is a function listed under the Mathematical category when we use the Function Wizard (Insert → Function). Because of its utility, the function has a graphical interface.

SUBTOTAL, gets the total/adds the data arranged in array-that is, a group of cells with labels for columns and/or rows.

For increasing the efficiency, we can choose up to three groups of arrays to which the function can be applied.

19. (i) There are 5 records and 6 fields in the table APPLICANTS.

(ii) (a) `SELECT NAME, FEE, GENDER, JOINYEAR FROM APPLICANTS WHERE JOINYEAR < 2010;`

(b) `SELECT NAME FROM APPLICANTS ORDER BY JOINYEAR;`

(c) `SELECT * FROM APPLICANTS WHERE GENDER = "F";`

Common Mistake	Students got confused in statement to display the details of female candidates they do not use asterisk (*) in query and only use GENDER column's name.

20. (i) DML provides various commands used to access and manipulate data in existing database. This manipulation involves inserting data into database tables, retrieving existing data, deleting data from existing tables and modifying existing data.

(ii) (a) **SELECT** Used to retrieve data from a database.

(b) **INSERT** Used to insert data into a table.

(c) **UPDATE** Used to update existing data within a table.

21. The following steps should be taken by the plant:

- **Conduct Safety Training** Regularly train employees on proper handling and emergency procedures for hazardous materials.
- **Provide Personal Protective Equipment (PPE)**: Ensure all workers have and use appropriate PPE, such as gloves, goggles, and protective clothing.
- **Implement Safety Protocols** Establish and enforce clear safety protocols, including proper labelling and storage of chemicals.
- **Install Safety Equipment** Equip the workplace with emergency showers, eyewash stations, and spill containment kits.
- **Regular Safety Audits** Conduct regular safety audits and risk assessments to identify and mitigate potential hazards.
- **Promote a Safety Culture** Encourage a culture of safety where employees feel responsible for their own and others' safety and can report hazards without fear of reprisal.

SQP Code : **PB-9/10** Series *i*-**Succeed 9-25/10** Roll No.

Sample Question Paper 09

Information Technology 10th (Code 402)

General Instructions

Time : 2 Hrs.

Max. Marks : 50

1. Please read the instructions carefully.
2. This Question Paper consists of 21 questions in two sections: Section A & Section B.
3. Section A has Objective Type Questions whereas Section B contains Subjective Type Questions.
4. Out of the given (5 + 16 = 21) questions, a candidate has to answer (5 + 10 = 15) questions in the allotted (maximum) time of 2 hours.
5. All questions of a particular section must be attempted in the correct order.
6. **Section A** Objective Type Questions (24 Marks)
   (i) This section has 5 questions.
   (ii) Marks allotted are mentioned against each question/part.
   (iii) There is no negative marking.
   (iv) Do as per the instructions given.
7. **Section B** Subjective Type Questions (26 Marks)
   (i) This section has 16 questions.
   (ii) A candidate has to do 10 questions.
   (iii) Do as per the instructions given.
   (iv) Marks allotted are mentioned against each question/part.

Section A Objective Type Questions *(24 Marks)*

1. Answer any 4 out of the given 6 questions based on Employability Skills. (4 × 1 = 4)

(i) What is a file?

(a) A file is a section of main storage used to store data.

(b) A file is a collection of information that has been given a name and have an extension.

(c) A file is the part of a program that is used to describe what the program should do.

(d) A file can be saved only in CDs.

(ii) In .... , we change from our normal activities to silence.

(a) meditation (b) stress
(c) worries (d) survival

(iii) .... is a common response to danger in all people and animals.

(a) Internal stress
(b) Environmental stress
(c) Survival stress
(d) Fatigue related stress

(iv) Effective communication involves

(a) Speaking only
(b) Listening only
(c) Speaking and listening
(d) Writing and reading

(v) To find a suitable market an entrepreneur performs the functions of

(a) advertisement and publicity
(b) appointment of selling agents
(c) new organisation structure
(d) Both (a) and (b)

(vi) What is the meaning of sustainable development?

(a) Development that focuses on economic growth only.

(b) Development that meets the needs of the present without compromising future generations.

(c) Development that prioritizes social progress over environmental protection.

(d) Development that relies solely on renewable energy sources.

2. Answer any 5 out of the given 6 questions. (5 × 1 = 5)

(i) .... include fonts, alignment, borders, background, number formats (for example, currency, date, number) and cell protection in document.

(a) Cell style (b) Numbering style
(c) Paragraph style (d) Character style

(ii) When you apply a .... , you apply a group of formatting effects together in one single step.

(a) effect (b) template
(c) style (d) format

(iii) Which shortcut key is used to make the selected text italic?

(a) Ctrl + I (b) Shift + I
(c) F1 + I (d) None of these

(iv) Line or paragraph spacing is measured in terms of lines or points, which is referred as ....

(a) text wrapping (b) PDF
(c) XPS (d) leading

(v) Which tab is used to create Table of Contents in a document?

(a) File tab (b) Format tab
(c) Insert tab (d) Styles tab

(vi) What dialog box opens on choosing File → Templates → Manage Templates in Writer?

(a) The File dialog box
(b) The Manage Templates dialog box
(c) The Templates dialog box
(d) The Record Template dialog box

3. Answer any 5 out of the given 6 questions. (5 × 1 = 5)

(i) Select .... → Track changes → Record from the menu bar. Thereafter, every change you record on the Calc will have a red border around it.

(a) File (b) Edit
(c) Format (d) Layout

(ii) Calc considers any data that it does not recognise as a number, date, time or formula, as:

(a) Expression (b) Equation
(c) Text (d) Function

(iii) State True or False.
'Goal seek in Calc, helps us to find the desired result by adjusting an input value.'

(a) True (b) False

(iv) Rajiv was asked to highlight the cells with green colour where the value entered is either greater than or equals to 120 in the worksheet containing thousands of data entries. Which feature of Calc should he use to get this work done within seconds?

(a) Conditional formatting
(b) Filtering
(c) Sorting
(d) Simple formatting

(v) Which of the following tools will help Swati, if she wants to arrange the height of students in her class in ascending order ?

(a) Ordering data (b) Sorting data
(c) Presenting data (d) Referring data

(vi) Rinky wants to know about the Number data type in Calc. Which of the following statement(s) is/are TRUE about it?

(a) Numbers are generally raw numbers or dates.

(b) Numbers can be started with a dollar sign ($) or with some other currency symbols to display as currency.

(c) By default, number and date data is aligned to the right in Calc.

(d) All of the above

4. Answer any 5 out of the given 6 questions. (5 × 1 = 5)

(i) When you define a field for a table, in which of the following parameters do access always considered optional?

(a) Field name (b) Data type
(c) Field size (d) Description

(ii) A ...... is a language that enables users to access and manipulate data in a database.

(a) DML (b) DCL
(c) TCL (d) DDL

(iii) Akshat wants to store a huge amount of information about his firm in a database. Which type of table organisation would be most suitable for this purpose?

(a) Relational
(b) Flat file
(c) Either relational or flat file
(d) Hierarchical

(iv) .... are the ways to produce the data stored in databases and tables in a printed form.

(a) Forms (b) Queries
(c) Reports (d) Data

(v) If the two departments (HR and IT) access the data simultaneously then only one department will see the updates by the other department. DBMS solves this issue. Thus, DBMS helps to avoid.............. which means if a single database is used by multiple users then it also ensures that the same data is present for all the users.

(a) Data redundancy
(b) Data inconsistency
(c) Data piracy
(d) Data modification

(vi) How much space does the DATE / TIME data type hold in Base?

(a) 2 bytes (b) 4 bytes
(c) 8 bytes (d) 10 bytes

5. Answer any 5 out of the given 6 questions. (5 × 1 = 5)

(i) What color is typically used for indicating the ground wire in electrical wires?

(a) Red
(b) Black
(c) Green or green with yellow stripe
(d) Blue

(ii) Which of the following falls in the category of workplace emergency?

(a) Earthquake
(b) Tornadoes
(c) Both (a) and (b)
(d) None of these

(iii) Do not use the elevator in times of fire in the building. Always use.............. for such emergencies.

(a) office space
(b) washroom
(c) staircase
(d) None of the above

(iv) Which of the following is considered a physical hazard in the workplace?

(a) Loud noise (b) Slippery floor
(c) Flickering light (d) Excessive heat

(v) Which type of fire extinguisher is suitable for Class A fires?

(a) Water extinguisher
(b) CO_2 extinguisher
(c) Foam extinguisher
(d) Dry Powder extinguisher

(vi) You should conduct regular fire drills in order to

(a) Eliminate workplace hazards
(b) Prepare for emergencies
(c) Carry out the risk assessment
(d) None of the above

Section B Subjective Type Questions *(26 Marks)*

Answer any 3 out of the given 5 questions on Employability skills. (3 × 2 = 6)

Answer each question in 20-30 words.

6. What is fatigue related stress? Why is it difficult to avoid?
7. In what way does inadequate planning hinder effective communication?
8. What is an operating system?
9. How can individuals acquire green skills?
10. What is the contribution of the entrepreneurs in the execution of Government policies?

Answer any 4 out of the given 6 questions in 20-30 words each. (4 × 2 = 8)

11. What do you mean by template?
12. What is the difference between absolute and relative hyperlinks as used in Calc?
13. What is the role of a foreign key in a database management system (DBMS)?
14. What is macro?
15. What are the advantages of having safer and healthy workplace?
16. Explain three conditions following which evacuation is done.

SP-09

Answer any 3 out of the given 5 questions in 50-80 words each. (3 × 4 = 12)

17. Rita is working in spreadsheet. She wants to know about the use of the following terms:

    (a) Quick Sort (b) Filtering Data

18. Differentiate between Save and Save As options.
19. Consider the following table PRODUCT

TABLE: PRODUCT

S_NO	P_Name	S_Name	Qty	Cost	City
S1	Biscuit	Priyagold	120	12.00	Delhi
S2	Bread	Britannia	200	25.00	Mumbai
S3	Chocolate	Cadbury	350	40.00	Mumbai
S4	Sauce	Kissan	400	45.00	Chennai

(i) How many fields and records are there in PRODUCT table?

(ii) Write SQL queries for the following:

(a) Display all Products whose Qty is between 100 and 400.

(b) Display S_Name, P_Name, Cost for all the Products whose Qty is less than 300.

(c) Display all the records alphabetically by S_Name.

20. Shubham is learning about DBMS. He wants to know about the following:

    (a) The purpose of DBMS

    (b) Any two uses of DBMS

21. Explain some of the ways to remove workplace hazards.

Answers in Topper's Style

My Commitment *I affirm that I am reviewing these solutions only after I have solved the Sample Question Paper 9 on my own. My purpose of looking the solutions is solely to verify whether my answers/solutions were correct or not and to identify my mistakes in case my solutions were wrong or I could not solve that.*

1. (i) (b) (ii) (a) (iii) (c) (iv) (c) (v) (d) (vi) (b)
2. (i) (a) (ii) (c) (iii) (a) (iv) (d) (v) (c) (vi) (c)
3. (i) (b) (ii) (c) (iii) (a) (iv) (a) (v) (b) (vi) (d)
4. (i) (d) (ii) (a) (iii) (a) (iv) (c) (v) (b) (vi) (c)
5. (i) (c) (ii) (c) (iii) (c) (iv) (b) (v) (a) (vi) (b)
6. Fatigue related stress builds up over a long time and can take a heavy toll on our body. It is caused by working too long or too hard at our job, school or home. It can also be caused by exercising too much or too long. If you do not know how to manage your time well or how to take time out for rest and relaxation, you will become a victim of fatigue related stress. It is difficult to avoid because many people feel that it is out of their control.
7. Poor planning act as a barrier to communication as without adequate planning the result desired due to the communication may not be achieved. So, we need to properly plan what message we want to send before actually sending it.
8. Operating system is the system software that performs all the basic tasks of a computer system. It works like an interface between the user and the computer hardware resources. It is a collection of programs that controls and coordinates the execution of all other tasks and functions in a computer system.

   It mainly provides an environment to run the software and serves services to the computer hardware.
9. Individuals can acquire green skills through education and training programs focused on sustainability, attending workshops, gaining practical experience, and staying updated with environmental developments.
10. The entrepreneurs provide an important contribution in implementing government policies and achieving the national goals.They cooperate with the government for implementations of development plans of the country.
11. A template is a collection of styles that already has some formatting in place, such as fonts, logos and line spacing and can be used as a starting point for almost anything that you want to create. Microsoft Word offers hundreds of free templates, including invoices, resumes, invitations and form letters, among others.
12. Hyperlinks can be stored within your file as either relative or absolute. An absolute link will stop working only if the target is moved. A relative link will stop working only if the start and target locations change relative to each other. For instance, if you have two spreadsheets in the same folder linked to each other and you move the entire folder to a new location, a relative hyperlink will not break but an absolute link will break.
13. In a DBMS, a foreign key establishes a relationship between two tables. It references the primary key of another table, enforcing referential integrity. It ensures data consistency by preventing actions that would violate the defined relationships, such as deleting a record referenced by a foreign key constraint.
14. A macro is a saved sequence of commands or keystrokes that are stored for later use. An example of a simple macro is one that "types" your address. The Open Office macro language is very flexible, allowing automation of both simple and complex tasks. Macros are especially useful to repeat a task the same way over and over again.
15. The advantages of having safer and healthy workplaces are as follows:
    (i) They have fewer days lost, therefore they have higher productivity.
    (ii) They can increase efficiency and quality, because they have healthier workplace.
16. Any three conditions following which evacuation is done are
    (i) In the event of a fire, an immediate evacuation is to be followed by the employees.
    (ii) In case of tornadoes, earthquakes, floods or explosions, the type of building can be a major factor in taking decision to follow the evacuation plan.
17. (a) Quick Sort is especially useful when you add new information to a spreadsheet. When a spreadsheet is long, it is usually easier to add new information at the bottom of the sheet, rather than adding it in its correct place.
    After you have added information, you can sort the records to update the spreadsheet and put the information in its correct place in quick sort.

    (b) When a sheet contains a large amount of data, it can be difficult to find information quickly. In that case, Filters can be used to narrow down the data in your worksheet, allowing you to view only the information you need.

In other words, Filters help you to ask questions to your data and retrieve only the relevant information filtering away the un-desirable data.

18. 'Save' means the file gets saved under its current name, in whatever folder it was saved before or in the default folder of that computer, whereas 'Save As' gives you the opportunity to save the file under a different name and in another folder. 'Save As' allows you to name the updated version with a new name and at the same time preserving the old version.

19. (i) There are 6 fields and 4 records in the table PRODUCT.

(ii) (a) `SELECT* FROM PRODUCT WHERE Qty BETWEEN 100 AND 400;`

(b) `SELECT S_Name, P_Name, Cost FROM PRODUCT WHERE Qty <300;`

(c) `SELECT * FROM PRODUCT ORDER BY S_Name;`

20. (a) DBMS (Database Management System) is used to store logically related information at a centralised location. It facilitates data sharing among all the applications requiring it.

(b) Two uses of database management system are as follows :

(i) DBMS is used to store data at a centralised location.

(ii) It is used to minimise data redundancy and data inconsistency.

21. Some of the ways to eliminate workplace hazards are as follows

(i) Remove damaged electrical outlets, cords, cables, etc.

(ii) Check overloaded outlets and circuits.

(iii) Combustible substances in unsecured locations, (including excessive trash and recycling) - keep these far from electrical equipment.

(iv) Clear all fire exit obstacles.

(v) Keep workspace and equipment clean, dry and well-ventilated and especially clean of oil and dust.

(vi) Follow workspace protocol and guidelines to ensure safety and health; know and understand rules and procedures concerning fire emergencies.

(vii) Ensure that smoke alarms and sprinkler systems are installed, working properly and are not blocked.

(viii) Conduct regular fire drills.

SQP Code : **PB-10/10** Series ***i*-Succeed 10-25/10** Roll No. | | | | | | | | |

Sample Question Paper 10

Information Technology 10th (Code 402)

General Instructions

Time : 2 Hrs.

Max. Marks : 50

1. Please read the instructions carefully.
2. This Question Paper consists of 21 questions in two sections: Section A & Section B.
3. Section A has Objective Type Questions whereas Section B contains Subjective Type Questions.
4. Out of the given (5 + 16 = 21) questions, a candidate has to answer (5 + 10 = 15) questions in the allotted (maximum) time of 2 hours.
5. All questions of a particular section must be attempted in the correct order.
6. **Section A** Objective Type Questions (24 Marks)
   (i) This section has 5 questions.
   (ii) Marks allotted are mentioned against each question/part.
   (iii) There is no negative marking.
   (iv) Do as per the instructions given.
7. **Section B** Subjective Type Questions (26 Marks)
   (i) This section has 16 questions.
   (ii) A candidate has to do 10 questions.
   (iii) Do as per the instructions given.
   (iv) Marks allotted are mentioned against each question/part.

Section A Objective Type Questions *(24 Marks)*

1. Answer any 4 out of the given 6 questions based on Employability Skills. (4 × 1 = 4)

(i) Identify the measure to protect computer from viruses.
(a) Sharing password with friends
(b) Allow anyone to use your device
(c) Use Antivirus
(d) Leave computer without logging out

(ii) Stress is identified as a condition in which a person is ....
(a) tensed
(b) worried
(c) relaxed
(d) Both (a) and (b)

(iii) .... is our body's way of responding to any kind of demand.
(a) Stress
(b) Self-regulation
(c) Self-motivation
(d) All of the above

(iv) What is the purpose of active listening?
(a) To interrupt the speaker and share your own thoughts
(b) To fully understand the speaker's message and respond appropriately
(c) To ignore the speaker and focus on other tasks
(d) To dominate the conversation and assert your authority

(v) Which of the following is a problem related to sustainable development?
(a) Overconsumption and waste production
(b) Efficient use of resources
(c) Promotion of renewable energy
(d) Conservation of biodiversity

(vi) Innovation of an entrepreneur includes
(a) division of work
(b) opening new markets
(c) introducing new products
(d) Both (b) and (c)

2. Answer any 5 out of the given 6 questions. (5 × 1 = 5)

(i) Template is a .... document based on which one can create a new document.
(a) blueprint (b) printed
(c) suggested (d) copied

(ii) Grouping drawing object can be used for which of the following?
(a) Combining drawing objects as one
(b) Resizing
(c) Adding more drawing objects
(d) None of the above

(iii) State True or False.
"A custom style displays user-defined styles."
(a) True (b) False

(iv) The Show Changes dialog box has which of the following settings?
(a) Data (b) Comment
(c) Views (d) All of these

(v) Rishabh wants to make a professional resume. He tried many a times but the end result was not satisfactory as he was not knowing what all points should be there and that too in which order . Which one of the following writer would you suggest him, so that his problem is solved?
(a) Template
(b) Form
(c) Worksheet
(d) Format

(vi) A new text document can be created by
(a) File → Open
(b) File → New → Text Document
(c) Open → New → Create
(d) None of the above

3. Answer any 5 out of the given 6 questions. (5 × 1 = 5)

(i) Shalini is working in a school. She is the class teacher of VIII B. It is the time to enter the subject marks and grades of all students of her class in a worksheet. While entering the marks and grades, she has to scroll up again and again to the row where all subject names are entered, in order to avoid any mistakes in her entries. This process is consuming a lot of her time. Help her by letting her know about one such tool by which she can fix the field rows from the following and continue with her work without wasting much time.
(a) Fix row (b) Fix column
(c) Freeze panes (d) Freeze all

(ii) According to LibreOffice Calc which of the following is not a What-if analysis tool?
(a) Conditional formatting
(b) Goal seek
(c) Scenarios
(d) Solver

(iii) ...... allows multiple users to view, edit and change in a Calc.
(a) Opening (b) Reviewing
(c) Sharing (d) Collaborating

(iv) Manya has created a spreadsheet using Calc, to find the average of the values in a range of cells. She wants to use a function, so that it is calculated automatically and also she can copy the same formula for other range of cells. Which of these functions will give the correct result?
(a) AVG (b) Average
(c) Mean (d) None of these

(v) Goal Seek is also called as............is one of the What-if analysis tools that is available in Calc.

(a) back-solving (b) solver
(c) forward-solving (d) result analysis

(vi) It refers to a cell or a range of cells on a worksheet and can be used to find the values or data that you want formula to calculate.

(a) Row (b) Column
(c) Autosum (d) Cell reference

4. Answer any 5 out of the given 6 questions. (5 × 1 = 5)

(i) Which of the following is not a good choice as a field name for a database?

(a) Emp_Id (b) Emp_dept
(c) Emp_name (d) Emp_set

(ii) The data in the data source is organised in

(a) text form (b) image form
(c) tabular form (d) paragraph form

(iii) Which of the following is not an object of a database?

(a) Report (b) Forms
(c) Query (d) Functions

(iv) Aanya is making a table in Database to store data of all the employees working in her organisation. She has decided on the various information that she needs to store in that table. She also has to have a field in which only unique data can be entered. Out of the given fields suggest the best field suitable that can be used as a primary key, so that it can accept only unique data.

(a) Emp_name (b) Emp_dept
(c) Emp_number (d) Emp_DOB

(v) Which data type is the most appropriate to store a short bio about an employee?

(a) Text (b) String
(c) Memo (d) Large text

(vi) When primary key constraint is applied on more than one column, then it is known as

(a) composite primary key
(b) foreign key
(c) composite foreign key
(d) connecting key

5. Answer any 5 out of the given 6 questions. (5 × 1 = 5)

(i) Which of the following is not mandatory to keep the good health of an employee?

(a) Cleanliness
(b) Food court
(c) Clean and fresh air
(d) Clean washroom

(ii) What are the potential causes of hazards at workplace?

(a) Poor ventilation
(b) Poor lighting
(c) Poor housekeeping
(d) All of the above

(iii) Do not wear ________ when working with machines.

(a) jewellery (b) safety glasses
(c) masks (d) gloves

(iv) If light is coming directly behind or in front of you then you may suffer from ________.

(a) eye strain
(b) sore eyes
(c) dry eyes
(d) eye strain and sore eyes

(v) What are the steps necessary for operating a fire extinguisher?

(a) Identify the safety pin of the fire extinguisher which is generally present in its handle
(b) Break the seal and pull the safety pin from the handle
(c) Use the fire extinguisher by squeezing the lever
(d) All of the above

(vi) If you have a safer and healthy workplace, there will be fewer days lost and it will have higher

(a) employee satisfaction
(b) productivity
(c) stress levels
(d) None of the above

Section B Subjective Type Questions *(26 Marks)*

Answer any 3 out of the given 5 questions on Employability Skills. $(3 \times 2 = 6)$

Answer each question in 20-30 words.

6. Why is self-regulation important in life?
7. Difference between file and folder.
8. Can you explain the principle of completeness in the context of effective communication?
9. What role do green skills play in addressing climate change?
10. Explain any two functions of an entrepreneur.

Answer any 4 out of the given 6 questions in 20-30 words each. $(4 \times 2 = 8)$

11. How can you define OLE?
12. What is the use of cell reference?
13. State any two ways of inserting sheets in a workbook?
14. How do you develop an evacuation policy and procedures?
15. What is Referential Integrity? Explain its purposes.
16. State any two practices for internet security.

SP-10

Answer any 3 out of the given 5 questions in 50-80 words each. $(3 \times 4 = 12)$

17. Lavish is preparing notes for his upcoming exams. Help him to write the correct answer of the following:
    (i) Scenario
    (ii) Absolute link
    (iii) Relative link
    (iv) Macro
18. Samarjit wants to know about template. Tell him the definition of template and also the steps to create a document using it.
19. Consider the following table: SHOPPE

TABLE: SHOPPE

Id	SName	Area
S001	ABC Computeronics	CP
S002	All Infotech Media	GK II
S003	Tech Shoppe	CP
S004	Geeks Tecno Soft	Nehru Place
S005	Hitech Tech Store	Nehru Place

(i) How many fields and records are there in SHOPPE table?
(ii) Write SQL commands for the following :
  (a) Display Id and SName of all the shops located in Nehru Place.
  (b) Display the details alphabetically by SName.
  (c) Display SName of shops whose Area is CP.

20. Your friend's father owns a restaurant. He manually enters the customers records in a register. You want to explain to him the importance of creating a database in computer. Tell the advantages of using computerized database with the help of the following points:
    (a) Data redundancy
    (b) Data inconsistency
    (c) Confidentiality
    (d) Sharing
21. Sanya is an HR manager at a mid-sized technology firm. Over the past year, several employees have reported experiencing eye strain, headaches, and other visual discomforts due to prolonged screen time. Sanya wants to implement strategies to reduce the risk of visual problems among her staff.

    What steps should Sarah tell her employees to reduce the risk of visual problems in her office environment?

Answers *in Topper's Style*

My Commitment *I affirm that I am reviewing these solutions only after I have solved the Sample Question Paper 10 on my own. My purpose of looking the solutions is solely to verify whether my answers/solutions were correct or not and to identify my mistakes in case my solutions were wrong or I could not solve that.*

1. (i) (c), (ii) (d), (iii) (a), (iv) (b), (v) (a), (vi) (d)
2. (i) (a), (ii) (a), (iii) (a), (iv) (d), (v) (a), (vi) (b)
3. (i) (c), (ii) (a), (iii) (c), (iv) (b), (v) (a), (vi) (d)
4. (i) (d), (ii) (c), (iii) (d), (iv) (c), (v) (a), (vi) (a)
5. (i) (b), (ii) (d), (iii) (a), (iv) (d), (v) (d), (vi) (b)
6. Self-regulation is important in life due to following reasons:
   (i) Self-regulation allows you to keep a tab on your own emotions.
   (ii) Self-regulation enables to develop the idea about 'what is appropriate behaviour' and 'what is inappropriate behaviour' in a given social condition.
   (iii) It helps in controlling negative impulses and reciprocate emotions for actualising set goals.
7. Differences between file and folder are as follows

File	Folder
Files may or may not have extensions.	Folders do not have extensions.
A file cannot contain another file/folder.	A folder can contain any number of file/folders.
A file has certain size and memory consumption.	A folder has no size of its own. It derives the size from the files it contains.
Files cannot be shared on network on their own.	Folders can be shared on network.

8. The principle of completeness implies that the message must be complete, means that it should convey all the information required by the receiver. Nothing which may be required by the receiver should be left out of the message.
9. Green skills are essential for developing and implementing climate change mitigation and adaptation strategies, including renewable energy deployment, energy efficiency improvements, and sustainable land use practices.
10. Two functions of an entrepreneur are as follows :
   (i) **Innovation** It includes introducing new products, opening new markets, new sources of raw material and new organisation structure.
   (ii) **Risk-taking** Choosing one among various alternatives, the end results of which are unpredictable.
11. Use an OLE **(Object Linking and Embedding)** object to insert in a presentation either a new document or an existing one. Embedding inserts a copy of the object and details of the source program in the target document, that is the program which is associated to the file type in the operating system. The major benefit of an OLE object is that it is quick and easy to edit the contents just by double-clicking on it. You can also insert a link to the object that will appear as an icon rather than an area showing the contents itself.
12. In order to avoid writing the data again and again for calculating purpose, cell reference is used. When you write any formula, for specfic function, you need to direct Excel the specific location of that data. This location is referred as, cell reference. So, everytime a new value added to the cell, the cell will calculate according to the reference cell formula.
13. Two ways of inserting sheets in a workbook are as follows :
   Select **Insert** → **Sheet** from the Menu Bar.
   Right-click on the sheet tab and click on **Insert Sheet.**
14. Each organization should have its own evacuation procedures. An evacuation policy should be made by assessing risks, defining roles, creating clear procedures, conducting regular drills, ensuring communication systems, and continuously reviewing and updating the plan for effectiveness.
15. Referential Integrity is a property of data stating that all its references are valid. In the context of relational databases, it is required that if a value of one attribute of a relation references a value of another attribute, then the referenced value must exist.
   Referential integrity is a database concept that is used to build and maintain logical relationships between two tables. It helps to maintain the accuracy and consistency of data in RDMS.
16. Any two practices for internet security are:
   (i) **Use Strong Passwords** A strong password is a combination of alpha-numeric and special characters. Do not use your mobile number, friends name, etc. for a password. Change your password frequently at least once in 2 or 3 weeks.
   (ii) **Backup Your Data** Always keep copies of your personal data in CDs, pendrive, etc. This may be helpful in a loss of data situation.
17. (i) The Scenario is a tool to test "What-if" questions. Each scenario is named and can be edited and

formatted separately. When you print the spreadsheet, only the contents of the currently active scenario are printed.

(ii) An absolute link contains all the information necessary to locate a resource and will stop working only if the target is moved.

(iii) A relative link locates a resource using an absolute URL as starting point will stop working only if the start and target locations change relative to each other.

(iv) A macro is a saved sequence of commands or keystrokes that are stored for later use or to be used repeatedly.

18. A template is a document model that you use to create other documents. For example, you can create a template for business reports that has your company's logo on the first page. New documents created from this template will all have your company's logo on the first page. Templates can contain anything that regular documents can contain, such as text, graphics, a set of styles and user-specific setup information such as measurement units, language, the default printer, and toolbar and menu customization.

To use a template to create a document:

(i) From the main menu, choose File→New→ Templates and Documents. The Templates and Documents dialog box will open.

(ii) In the box on the left, click the Templates icon if it is not already selected. A list of template folders appears in the center box.

(iii) Double-click the folder that contains the template that you want to use. A list of all the templates contained in that folder appears in the center box.

(iv) Select the template that you want to use. You can preview the selected template or view the template's properties:

(a) To preview the template, click the Preview icon. A preview of the template appears in the box on the right.

(b) To view the template's properties, click the Document Properties icon. (For the location of the Document Properties icon) The template's properties appear in the box on the right.

(v) Click Open. The Templates and Documents dialog box closes and a new document based on the selected template opens in Writer. You can then edit and save the new document just as you would any other document.

19. (i) There are 3 fields and 5 records in the table SHOPPE.

(ii) (a) `SELECT Id, SName FROM SHOPPE WHERE Area='Nehru Place';`

(b) `SELECT * FROM SHOPPE ORDER BY SName;`

(c) `SELECT SName FROM SHOPPE WHERE Area='CP';`

20. (a) Data redundancy means duplication of data computerised database avoids duplication of data and ensures that there is only one instance of certain data.

(b) Data inconsistency helps, if a single database is used by multiple users then it ensures that the same data is present for all the users.

(c) The DBMS can ensure different views for the different users of the database. This keeps the confidentiality of the data safe.

(d) Different users can use the same database to access the data according to their needs. Hence, DBMS provides sharing of data and resources.

21. To reduce the risks of visual problems:

- Adjust the brightness of computer screen to save your eyes from strain.
- Reposition the screen to avoid glare from lights or windows.
- Keep a proper vision distance from computer screen and blink your eyes in an interval.
- Wear anti-glare glasses while working in computer.
- Keep the screen clean and use a desk lamp to make it easier to see.
- Ensure the screen colours are easy to look at, and that the characters are sharp and legible.

SP-10

Knowledge Booster Zone

Welcome to the Knowledge Booster Zone !

This section is dedicated to enhancing your understanding of key concepts. Here, you will find chapter-wise revision notes designed to solidify your **foundational knowledge**. Use these notes to review and reinforce what you've learned, ensuring you're well-prepared for each topic.

Progress Tracker Tick the papers as you complete them.

- ☐ Communication Skills-II
- ☐ Self Management Skills-II
- ☐ ICT Skills-II
- ☐ Entrepreneurial Skills-II
- ☐ Green Skills-II
- ☐ Digital Documentation (Advanced)
- ☐ Electronic Spreadsheet (Advanced)
- ☐ Database Management System
- ☐ Maintain Health, Safety and Secure Working Environment

Part A (Employability Skills)

Chapter 1 Communication Skills-II

The word communication comes from the Latin word **communicare** meaning **to share**. Being able to communicate effectively is one of the most important life skills.

There are three important parts of communication.

- **Transmission** The sender transmits the message to the receiver through a medium.
- **Receiver** The receiver gets the message and interprets it into meaningful information.
- **Feedback** The feedback of this meaningful information is conveyed back to the sender to complete the communication cycle.

Methods of Communication

The methods or types of communication are described below:

Verbal Communication

Verbal communication means communication through spoken oral and written words. It implies use of words which make up a language. It is the ability to communicate using words in understandable language i.e. English, Hindi, French, Urdu etc.

Verbal communication are of two types. These are

- **Oral communication** It means communication through the mouth (speaking) and the ears (listening). Two individuals conversing with each other, either face-to-face or through the telephone is an example of oral communication.
- **Written communication** This is a medium of communication that entails the written word. Letters, e-mails, websites, memorandums, reports, notices, manuals, quotations, newsletters, newspapers etc., are forms of written communication.

Non-Verbal Communication

Non-verbal communication occurs without using any oral or written word. Instead, it relies on various non-verbal cues such as physical movements, colors, signs, symbols, body language etc., to express feelings, attitudes or information.

Various components or forms of non-verbal communication are

- Eye contact
- Facial expressions
- Gestures
- Body language
- Posture and body orientation
- Space and Distance
- Proximity
- Humour
- Touch
- Silences
- Visual communication
- Para-linguistic (tone/ pitch/ inflection)
- Personal appearance
- Symbols

Visual Communication

Visual communication conveys ideas and information in forms that can be seen. It is also known as **graphic communication**. It includes graphic design, illustration and animation, books, print, magazines, screen based media, interactive web design, motion graphics, short film, visual imagery for advertising and promotion, corporate identity and packaging design etc.

The Communication Cycle

The main steps in a communication form is communication cycle. These steps are shown and explained below

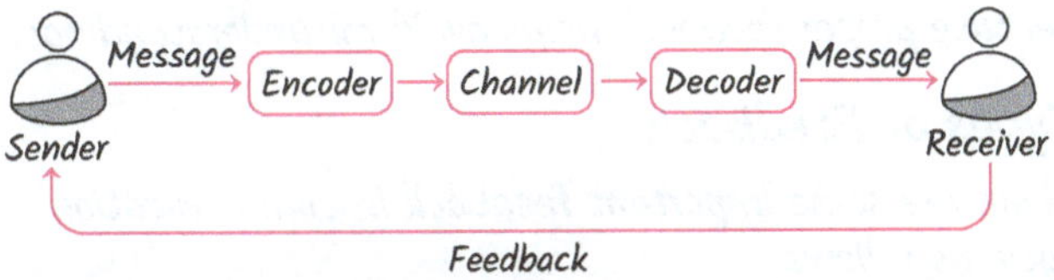

- The **Communicator** or **Sender** is the person or organisation originating the communication. It decides what the message is, how it will be expressed and sent, and who it is to be sent to.
- **Encoding** means to change the message into a form suitable for sending.

- The **Message** is the actual information that the sender wishes to convey to the receiver.
- The **Medium** or **Channel** is the means by which the message is sent. Some messages are more effective in written form, others may be more effective on the telephone (e.g. urgent messages), while others may be more effective if sent via electronic means such as e-mail.
- **Transmission** of message describes one-way, linear process in which a sender encodes a message and transmits it through a channel to a receiver who decodes it.
- The **Receiver** is the person or organisation to whom the message is sent.
- **Decoding** is the process in which the receiver interprets and understands the message.
- **Feedback** is the receiver's response to the message. Requesting clarification is part of a good feedback phase of a communication cycle. Without feedback, the communication cycle remains incomplete.

Meaning and Importance of Feedback

Feedback is the final step in the communication cycle. It is the receiver's response to the message, which enables the sender to evaluate the effectiveness of the message sent.

Thus, feedback plays a very important role in communication cycle. If there is absence of feedback then it will lead to a communication barrier.

For example, if the receiver doesn't understand the meaning of the message, the sender can know this by the feedback received and can improve the message accordingly.

For the feedback to be effective, it must be clear, well in time, specific, having the right attitude, true and honest, impersonal and informative. It is important because proper feedback helps avoid misunderstandings.

Types of Feedback

There are some important feedback in communication cycle as follows

1. **Descriptive Feedback** A descriptive feedback on the contrary, provides meaningful information in a detailed, expensive manner that also contains some analysis or suggestion etc.
2. **Specific Feedback** The specific feedback talks about a thing or particularly without talking about a general overview. e.g., I like the way you described your grandfather's character. It makes me feel like I know him too.
3. **Non-Specific Feedback** The non-specific feedback, on the other hand, talks about the entire think while giving a general overview. It does not particularly pinpoint is specific think/feature.
   e.g., I like your story. It is good.

Effective Communication

It is the process of exchanging ideas, thoughts, opinions, knowledge and data so that the message is received and understood with clarity and purpose. When we communicate effectively, both the sender and receiver feel satisfied.

Barriers to Effective Communication

Anything that prevents or disturbs the sending or receiving of a communication or message is considered as a barrier to communication. Speaking louder to drown out the noise is a measure to overcome a barrier to communication.

The types of barriers to effective communication include

Physical and Environment Based Barriers

These are environmental factors which prevent or reduce the sending and receiving of communications. They include physical distance, distracting noises and similar interferences.

Interpersonal Barriers

They arise from the judgements, emotions and social values of people. They cause a psychological distance between people similar to the physical distance. Thus, sometimes the message may not be understood at all. At other times, part of the communication is only understood. In other cases, the message may be wrongly interpreted.

Semantic Barriers

These refer to symbols or visuals used in the message. The barrier may arise due to the symbol we use, as it may mean different things to different people.

For example, the 'thumbs up' gesture is recognised as a sign of approval or agreement in European countries, but it may be interpreted as an indecent gesture in rural areas of India. Symbols are of the following three types:

- Linguistic or Related to Language
- Pictures
- Action

Intra-Personal Barriers

It refers to the elements within the individuals personality which acts as a barrier in receiving, analysing and interpreting the information that is available. There are different types of intra-personal barriers in an individuals's personality like selective perception, individual differences in communication skills, emotions, preconceived ideas etc.

Factors Causing Barriers

There are a number of factors which may cause the barriers to communication mentioned above. Very often the factors are related to culture, especially if the sender and receiver of the communication belong to different cultures.

Thus, the factors causing barriers to communication include:

- Poor Planning
- Mistrust
- Differences in Meaning/Ambiguity
- Distortion
- Implied Meaning
- Noise
- Absence of Feedback
- Time and Distance

Measures to Overcome Barriers

To ensure that barriers to communication do not arise or can be overcome, we can take some steps related to the factors causing the barriers. The steps to be taken for overcoming some of these factors are:

- **Be Prepared before Communicating** Often we are not properly prepared for communicating a message because we do not have enough information or knowledge of what we want to communicate.
- **Give Sufficient Time** The message should not be communicated too fast; this is particularly true for oral messages. If it is not done at a suitable speed the receiver may miss its important points or may not understand it at all.
- **Simplify the Language** Both the sender and receiver of the communication must have sufficient knowledge of the language in which they are communicating. If this is not confirmed, it is better to use simplified language with easily understood words and simple ideas.
- **Don't Assume Anything** Without appropriate feedback, the sender of the message should not assume that his message has been understood. He should only rely on suitable feedback about the understanding of the message.
- **Avoid Overconfidence** Have a humble attitude when communicating a message. Similarly, the receiver should not be egocentric, otherwise he may fail to understand some important points of the message he has received.
- **Preconceived Notions/Expectations, Perceptions and Assumptions** When the receiver has a different perception from that of the sender, communication is affected. This can be overcome by thinking from the speaker's point of view.
- **Avoid Making Judgements** Communication can fail if the message communicated passes some judgement against the receiver, as then the content of the message is not understood in its real sense. It makes the receiver defensive, thus creating a barrier. So, this kind of situation should be avoided.
- **Respect the Receiver** There should be mutual respect for each other by the sender and the receiver for a message to be successfully communicated. This will motivate each of them to take out some time for the other person.
- **Improve the Attitude** The receiver should not have apathy towards the sender and vice-versa, otherwise there will be a breakdown in communication.
- **Information Overload/ Attention Span** Overload of information or giving too many details reduces the receiver's ability to concentrate on the important parts of the message.

Principles of a Effective Communication

The most basic principle for a communication to be effective is that the intended message of the sender and the interpreted message of the receiver are one and the same. Although this should be the goal in any communication, it is not always achieved. Thus, a set of principles needs to be followed to ensure it. The most popular name of these basic principles is known as 7C's of Effective Communication.

The 7C's of Effective Communication

We communicate at home, at work, with our neighbour etc. We communicate in written or oral, audio or visual, so it is important that we follow the 7C's of effective communication.

These principles of effective communication are:

1. **Completeness** The message must be complete, meaning that it should convey all the information required by the receiver. Nothing which may be required by the receiver should be left out of the message. The sender of the message must take into consideration the requirements of the receiver while making the message.
2. **Conciseness** It means communicating what you want to convey in the least possible words so that there are no unnecessary bits of information in it. A concise communication is both time-saving as well as cost-saving.
3. **Consideration** The sender should have consideration for the receiver of the message while making the communication to be sent. The sender should focus on 'you' instead of 'I' or 'we'. The receiver's viewpoint, background, mindset, culture, educational level etc.,
4. **Concreteness** It implies being objective and clear, rather than vague, confused or obscure. A concrete message will have specific facts and figures.
5. **Clarity** It implies emphasising a specific message in a communication instead of trying to cover too many items in one communication. It makes understanding of the message easier by the receiver.
6. **Courtesy** A courteous message is politely worded. It implies that the message should use words which show the sender's respect for the receiver. Thus, the sender of the message should be sincerely polite and well-mannered.
7. **Correctness** It implies that there are no grammatical, spelling or punctuation errors in the communication being sent.

Basic Writing Skills

Writing skills are an important part of communication. Good writing skills allow you to communicate your message clearly and easily to a large audience.

we should understand some basic parts of a document such as **kinds of sentences, phrases, parts of a sentence, parts of speech** and **construction of a paragraph.**

The Sentence

A sentence is a set of words that is complete in itself and which contains a subject and a predicate part. It conveys a statement, question, exclamation or command. It consists of a main clause and sometimes one or more subordinate clauses.

Kinds of Sentence

There are four types of sentences. These are:

form	function	example sentence	final punctuation
Declarative	**statement** It tells us something	John likes Mary.	.
Interrogative	**question** It asks us something	Does Mary like John?	?
Imperative	**command** It tells us to do something	Stop! Close the door.	! or .
Exclamative	**exclamation** It expresses surprise	What a funny story he told us!	!

Phrases

Phrases are a group of words that work together to communicate an element of speech.

There are five types of phrases as

- Prepositional phrase
- Appositive phrase
- Participal phrase
- Gerund phrase
- Infinitive phrase

Parts of a Sentence

A sentence consists of two parts, a **subject part** and a **predicate part**. Each part of a sentence has a particular function, though sometimes both parts may not be written for it to be complete.

Parts of Speech

According to their function in a sentence, words in the English language are classified as different parts of speech.

These are disussed below:

- **Noun** It is a word for a person, place, thing or idea. Nouns are sometimes used with an article (the, a, an).

  Example The young <u>boy</u> brought me a very long <u>letter</u> from the <u>teacher</u>.

- **Pronoun** It is a word used in place of a noun. A pronoun is usually substituted for a specific noun, which is called its antecedent.

  Example Jagdish was in a hurry, so he washed the car himself.
- **Verb** In a sentence, the verb expresses an action or the state of the subject in the sentence.

  Example Jagdish was in a hurry, so he washed the car himself.
- **Adjective** It is a word used to modify or describe a noun or a pronoun.

  Example The young boy brought me a very long letter from the class teacher.
- **Adverb** It describes or modifies a verb, an adjective, or another adverb, but never a noun.

  Example She laughed loudly.
- **Preposition** It is a word placed before a noun or pronoun to link it to another word in the sentence.

  Example The mouse jumped off the table onto the floor of the room.
- **Conjunction** It joins words, phrases, or clauses and indicates the relationship between them.

  Example You can have either chocolate or vanilla ice-cream.
- **Interjection** It is a word used to express emotion. It is often followed by an exclamation mark.

  Example Oh God! I don't know what to do about this mess.

Articles

An article is a kind of adjective which is always used with a noun and gives some information about it. The words 'a' and 'an' are called indefinite articles because the noun they go with is indefinite or general. Instances of indefinite articles used in sentences are:

- I will reach home within an hour.
- It is difficult to find a one-rupee currency note in the present day.

The word "the" is known as a definite article because it refers to a specific noun.

Construction of a Paragraph

A paragraph is a group of sentences dealing with a particular topic. Paragraphs can be of any length and can vary from only one sentence to even more than ten sentences.

Chapter 2 Self Management Skills-II

Self-management, also referred to as **self-control**, is the ability to control one's emotions, thoughts and behaviour effectively in different situations. This also includes motivating oneself, and setting goals.

To perform well at work and life in general, you must be able to manage and improve yourself in various skills including discipline and timeliness, goal-setting, problem solving, teamwork, professionalism, etc.

Stress

Stress is identified as a condition in which a person is tensed and worried. It can affect both our body and our mind. The good stress is called 'Eustress', whereas the bad stress is termed as 'Distress'.

Stress Management

Stress management refers to focusing human efforts for maintaining a healthy body and mind capable of better with standing stressful situations. Stress refers to a physical, mental or emotional strain or tension. Small amount of stress have a positive effect and they help us stretch ourselves to a new level.

Importance of Stress Management

Stress management is critical for dealing with challenges and setbacks.

It helps people bounce back from failure and forge ahead.

- **For a better life** Learning stress management skills and applying them to everyday life helps a person take control of his or her life. Handling stress effectively builds a positive outlook. A solution oriented approach helps in overcoming problems and living a better life.
- **To improve health** Constantly being under stress affects your health. It makes you prone to various diseases and accelerates your aging process. Research shows that stressed individuals age faster than those who are stress free.
- **To enhance performance** Stress at work has become common in today's fast paced world. Workplace stress hampers one's ability to perform well and succeed. Workplace stress may lead to emotional burnout, low

self-esteem or a feeling of worthlessness.

It can also impact your career growth. Hence, believe in the importance of stress management in an organisation and take necessary steps to reduce stress.

- **To improve communication** Once you start handling stress, everything falls in place. Stress management starts untangling your problems. Your communication process improves. You open up more and try to express your feelings. Misunderstanding are cleared.

Stress Management Techniques

With proper planning and use of the right techniques, stress can be reduced or managed to remain within tolerable limits. These techniques have been well-known from quite some time and involve disciplined exercising as well as various relaxation techniques. They are shown in the diagram below:

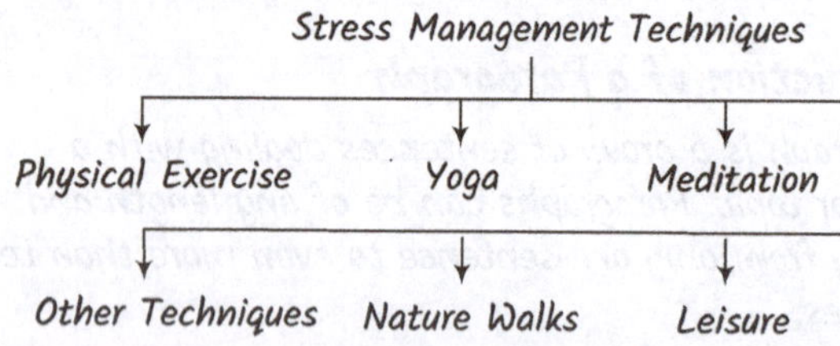

- **Physical Exercise** It is an activity done to achieve physical fitness and overall health. It improves blood circulation, lowers blood pressure, clears the mind of worrying thoughts, improves our self-image, makes us feel better about ourselves and increases social contact.
- **Yoga** Yoga is a mind-body practice that combines physical poses, controlled breathing and meditation or relaxation. It will help in stress management by relaxing the body and mind, develop a connection between the mind and the body, releasing emotional energy and helping to breathe more effectively.
- **Meditation** In meditation, we change from our normal activities to silence. We go beyond the noisy thoughts in the mind and enter a state of restful alertness. During meditation, although we are in a state of deep rest, our mind is fully alert and awake.
- **Leisure** This means spending holidays with your family and friends, travelling to other areas in the country or outside and any other similar activities. Leisure gives you the benefits of enabling you to indulge in your interests or hobbies, gives you a 'break' from stress, provides an outlet for relief and also provides social contact.
- **Nature Walks** It means walking in the local park or similar such activity. These walks may be done more than once a day for short periods of time during which we indulge in 'thought-stopping', i.e. not to think about our day-to-day activities.
- **Other Techniques** These include getting adequate sleep, which is a good stress reducer. When we wake refreshed after a night's sleep, we have adequate day time energy.

Ability to Work Independently

One of the abilities that we require to develop in us is that of working independently. For doing this, we have to become a self-aware, self-motivated and self-regulating independent person.

A good way to start becoming independent is by carefully thinking about our own learning style. We should find out whether

- We prefer working independently or we need a more structured environment to work efficiently.
- We are self-motivated or we need regular feedback in order to make progress in our work.
- We work best at our own pace or we need to be prodded by others to work faster.
- We know what it means to be independent.

Necessary Skills for Independent Working

From the above, we can understand that some skills are required for developing an independent working style. These are:

- Becoming self-aware, self-monitoring and self-correcting.
- Knowing what we need to do.
- Taking the initiative rather than waiting to be told what to do.
- Doing what is asked to the best of our ability, without the need for external prodding and working until the job is completed.

Self-awareness

Self-awareness refers to our knowledge and understanding of ourselves. It includes our emotions, beliefs, assumptions, biases, knowledge base, abilities, motivations, interests etc., So, we should make a conscious effort to learn about ourselves, i.e. our abilities, beliefs, likes and dislikes. The feeling of self-awareness enhances our self-confidence.

There are two types of self-awareness as follows

- **Internal Self-awareness** Internal self-awareness is about focusing on your inner values. The emotions, values, goals, aspirations, everything which we possess in our inner feelings. Behaviours, thoughts, our weaknesses and strength which help us present our views and feel in a certain way. These things come under the category of internal self-awareness.
- **External Self-awareness** External self-awareness deals with our feelings and behaviour with others. It is the ability to look at others. This awareness helps you decide what others think about you. If you can judge whether a person is happy with you or not, then you have better external self-awareness. It certainly makes a person more effective in paying attention to others.

Self-motivation

Self-motivation refers to your ability to identify effective methods of making yourself move from thinking about something to taking action about it. Everyone is different.

Some individuals are highly self-motivated while others require external deadlines or some type of reward or penalty in order to move from thought to action. Identifying your specific needs in this area is the first step.

Self-regulation

Self-regulation focuses on your ability to influence personal and professional improvement based on your self-awareness and motivation. Useful questions you should ask yourself in an effort to self-regulate yourself are:

- Who will directly supervise or guide in my project? With what frequency (daily, weekly etc.)?
- What are the deadlines, if any, relevant to my project?
- What are the requirements, if any, for my project? These might include progress reports, oral presentations, a final written report or any other documents?
- What are the outcomes that I desire from my participation in this project? What, if anything, do I need to do in order to achieve these outcomes?

Goal Setting

It is all about finding and listing your goals and then planning on how to achieve them. Goals allow you to separate out what's important.

It helps you to focus on the end result instead of less important work. This will make you successful in your career and personal life.

We can use SMART method to set goals. SMART stands for:

- **Specific** Well defined, clear, and unambiguous
- **Measurable** With specific criteria that measure your progress toward the accomplishment of the goal
- **Achievable** Attainable and not impossible to achieve
- **Realistic** Within reach, realistic, and relevant to your life purpose
- **Timely** With a clearly defined timeline, including a starting date and a target date. The purpose is to create urgency.

Time Management

Time management is the ability to plan and control how you spend the hours of your day well and do all that you want to do.

Steps for Effective Time Management are

- **Organize** Plan your day-to-day activities and make a timetable that you follow.
- **Priorities** You make a to-do list that has all your activities and you rank them in the order of importance. It helps you to get the most important task done first and also to track what is pending.
- **Control** You have a control over your activities and time.
- **Track** You identify and note where you have spent your time. This will help you analyse if you have used your time effectively or not. It also helps you to identify time-wasting activities

Chapter 3 ICT Skills-II

Introduction to Operating System

Operating System (OS) is the system software that performs all the basic tasks of a computer system. It works like an interface between the user and the computer hardware resources. It actually controls the execution of all the tasks that are performed in a computer.

"An operating system is a collection of programs that controls and coordinates all the tasks and functions in a computer system. It mediates between application programs and hardware components."

Types of Operating System

Types	Features
Time Sharing Operating System	• In this OS, a small amount of time is allocated for the processing simultaneously. • It provides scheduling to each process to be run on. e.g. Mac OS
Real-Time Operating System	• It was designed to respond to an event within a predetermined time. • It aims to execute real time applications such as auto pilot mechanism used in aircrafts. • It has very little user-interface capability and no end-user utilities. e.g. Windows CE, QNX, RTLINUX, Vx Works, Free RTOS, etc.
Single-User Operating System	• It is designed for one user to effectively use a computer at a time. e.g. Windows 95/NT/2000, DOS, etc.
Multi-User Operating System	• It allows many users to take advantage of the computer's resources simultaneously. • It ensures that problem with one user doesn't affect the entire community of users. e.g. Unix, VMS, Linux, Windows 2000, etc.
Single-Tasking Operating System	• It allows only a single program to run at a time. e.g. Palm OS, etc.
Multi-Programming Operating System	• It allows to run several programs at a time using time sharing. • This operating system keeps several jobs in memory at a time. e.g. Linux, Unix, etc.
Multi-Tasking Operating System	• This operating system is the logical extension of multi-programming operating system. • In this OS, more than one processes can be executed concurrently. • It reduces CPU idle time. e.g. Microsoft's Windows and Apple's Mac OS.
Distributed Operating System	• It uses multiple central processors to serve multiple real time applications. • It manages a group of independent computers and makes them appear to a single computer. • Data processing jobs are distributed among the processors according to their efficiency. e.g. LOCUS etc.
Batch-Processing Operating System	• Similar types of jobs are grouped under batch and these batches are executed without user's interruption. • Jobs are processed in the order of submission, i.e. on First Come First Serve (FCFS) basis. e.g. DOS, IBM OS/2, etc.
Multi-Processing Operating System	• Use of two or more CPUs within a single computer system. • Simultaneous processing of two or more programs by multiple processors. e.g. Linux, Unix, Windows 2000, etc.

Operating Systems for Desktop and Laptop

Some commonly used operating systems for desktop and laptop are as follows :

UNIX

It is an operating system which was first developed in the 1969s. UNIX systems have a Graphical User Interface (GUI) similar to different Microsoft Windows which provides an easy way to use platform. It supports fully multi-tasking with protected memory which means multiple users can run multiple programs at the same time without interfering with each other or crashing the system.

UNIX was one of the first operating system to be written in a high level programming language, namely C. This meant that it could be installed on virtually any computer for which a C compiler existed. This natural portability combined with its low price made it a popular choice among universities.

Linux

It is an open source operating system designed primarily for the PCs and laptops. Linux was designed considering Unix compatibility. Its functionality list is quite similar to that of Unix. One of the most valued advantage of Linux over the other platforms lies with the high security levels. It is a virus free operating system.

Mac OS (Apple Macintosh)

It is an operating system which was introduced on March 24, 2001 by Apple Inc and was initially named as system software, which was later renamed as Mac OS. Most recent version of OS is based on Unix because it has a good graphical interface.

MS-Windows

It is a series of Graphical User Interface (GUI) operating systems developed, marketed and sold by Microsoft. Microsoft introduced an operating environment named Windows on November 20, 1985 as an add-on to MS-DOS in response to the growing interest in Graphical User Interfaces (GUIs). The most popular versions of Windows for personal computers, mobile devices and server computers are as follows :

Windows NT, Windows 95, Windows 98, Windows 2000, Windows ME, Windows XP, Windows Vista, Windows 7, Windows 8, Windows 10.

Solaris

It is a free operating system originally developed by Sun Microsystems in 1993. Oracle Solaris, as it is now known and owned by Oracle Corporation since Oracle's acquisitions of Sun in January 2010.

MS-DOS (Microsoft-Disk Operating System)

It is an operating system that runs on PC and developed by IBM corporation in 1981. It was the most commonly used member of the DOS family of operating system.

Initially, MS-DOS was targeted at Intel 8086 processors running on computer hardware using floppy disks to store and access not only the operating system, but application software and user data as well.

Operating Systems for Mobile Phone and Tablets

It is an OS that operates on smartphones, tablets and digital mobile devices.

The most common operating systems for mobile phone and tablets are as follows :

Android

It is the most popular Linux based open source software developed by Google in September, 2008.

It is basically designed for touch screen mobile devices like tablets, smartphones, etc. Now-a-days, it is most common OS used in mobile phones.

iOS

It is the popular mobile operating system developed by Apple Incorporation. iOS was introduced on June 29, 2007 when the first iPhone was developed. This operating system is commonly used in Apple iPhone, iPod Touch, iPad, Second Generation Apple TV, etc.

BlackBerry

This is the most secure operating system used in leading smartphones developed by BlackBerry company. BlackBerry was introduced on January 19, 1999. It also supports WAP 1.2.

Symbian

It was developed on 5th June, 1997 and sold by Symbian Ltd. It is a mobile OS targeted at mobile phones that offer a high level of integration with communication and Personal Information Management (PIM) functionality.

User Interface

The user interface is one of the most important parts of any operating system because it allows users to easily access the applications and the hardware. It is set of commands or menus.

The user can interact with the computer by using mainly two kinds of interfaces:

- **Character User Interface (CUI)** This is a mechanism of interacting with a computer system or software by typing commands to perform specific tasks.
- **Graphical User Interface (GUI)** It is used as an interface between program and user. This is a computer program that enables a user to

communicate with a computer through the use of symbols, visual metaphors and pointing devices.

Menu, Icons and Taskbar on the Desktop

Let's discuss about Windows 10 operating system.

Windows 10

Windows 10 is a personal computer operating system developed and released by Microsoft in 2015. It is easy to use social media sites like Facebook and Twitter.

Desktop

Desktop is the main screen of the Windows 10 operating system. There are three components as Icons, taskbar and desktop background.

Icons An icon is a picture or graphic representation of an application or a file. If you want to open or access an icon, double click on it.

Taskbar The most important component of the desktop is Taskbar. By default, it is present at the bottom of the screen. Its parts are

- Start menu
- Opened program
- Notification area
- **Start Menu** To search for an application, you can also open the Start menu. An alphabetical list of all the applications installed on the computer appears. To open the Start menu, click on Start button.
- **Notification Area** It is located at the right side of the taskbar. It shows different types of notifications for your computer such as, your Internet connection or the volume level. By default, the notification area shows only a few icons but you can click the upward arrow on its left side to see the other options.

File Concept, File Operations, File Organisation, Directory Structures and File System Structures

Files can be separately placed into groups, called folders/directories. Each directory/folder can contain related files and/or sub-folders.

A sub-folder may contain one or more files and sub-folders within.

This allows easy accessibility of files. Files are managed in a hierarchy. This allows you to view the files in the current directory and then move to sub-directories.

Creating a Folder

The steps to create a new folder are as follows

Step 1. Double click on This PC.

Step 2. Select the drive in which you want to create a new folder.

Step 3. Window will open up showing files and folders in Local Disk.

Step 4. Click New folder on the toolbar.

Or

Right click anywhere in the blank area. A drop-down menu will appear. Select New → Folder.

Step 5. A new folder is created with name New Folder highlighted.

Step 6. Type a name for the folder.

Creating a File

To create a new file, steps are as follows:

Step 1. Right-click anywhere in the blank area.

Step 2. A drop down menu will appear. In the drop down menu, click New and select the type of the file you want to create.

Apply Basic Skills for Care and Maintenance of Computer

Importance and Need of Care and Maintenance of Computer

Computer systems require maintenance, so that the system works efficiently. Poor maintenance may lead to system failure.

Regular care and maintenance may help you detect any issues at an early stage and keep it functioning well.

Since, a lot of important data is stored in the computer, it is necessary to have regular maintenance of the computer to be done. Both internal and external parts of the computer system should be taken care of

1. Keep the computer dust free.
2. Do not eat or drink while working on the computer. Food or drink may spill on the system.
3. To keep the keyboard clean, make sure your hands are clean before using it.
4. CDs and DVDs should be handled carefully, so that it does not get any scratches.
5. Keep keyboard covered when not in use.

Cleaning the Computer Components

Computer components need proper care to last longer. Preventive maintenance increases the life of the components.

For example, a cable is damaged, but still working. It should be replaced or repaired immediately to prevent any other damage.

Let's discuss how to clean common peripheral devices of computer

Computer Monitor

To clean the computer monitor, you can use a soft lint-free cloth, like cotton and water or special cleaning liquid. You should not spray water or cleaning liquid directly on the computer monitor as it may run through the seams.

Keyboard

Dirt and dust can cause damage to the keyboard. Keys of the keyboard may not function properly, if dirt enters the keys. You should always clean the keyboard periodically by holding upside down and shaking it.

Optical Mouse

You can clean the bottom of the optical mouse with a clean lint-free cloth. Lens area can be cleaned by blowing air or cotton swab.

CDs and DVDs

Keep CD/DVD in proper case to prevent damage. If there is some dirt on the CD or DVD, it may not work at all. Finger prints and dirt can be removed by lightly rubbing with a clean lint-free cotton cloth.

Protecting Computer Against Viruses

A computer virus is a software program that attaches itself to other programs and alters their behavior. A virus may or may not be destructive.

Some viruses erase data or corrupt programs on the computer. VIRUS is an acronym for Vital Information Resources Under Seize.

A computer can get infected with virus in any of the following ways:

- infected files
- infected pen drives
- infected CD-ROMs/DVD-ROMs
- through infected file attachment of e-mails

A computer virus cannot do the following:

- it cannot infect files on CD or DVD, if they are closed for writing.
- it cannot infect computer hardware like, keyboard, mouse, etc.

The following points should be kept in mind to prevent virus infection:

- install and use anti-virus software
- keep anti-virus software updated
- scan all the files that you download from the Internet
- do not open e-mails of an unknown person/sender

Preparing Computer Against Virus

To prevent our computer from being infected with virus, we should install anti-virus software, run it periodically and keep it updated, so that it can scan and remove new viruses.

For an anti-virus program to be effective:

- it needs to run in the background at all times.
- keep the anti-virus software updated, so that it can recognize new viruses.
- run full disk scans periodically.

Firewall

A computer firewall could be a programmable device or a software or a network security system that monitors and controls incoming and outgoing network traffic based on user-defined security rules.

Firewalls enhance the security of computers connected to a network, such as LAN or the Internet. A firewall typically establishes a barrier between a trusted internal network and untrusted external network, such as the Internet.

Cookies

In computing, cookies are small files which are stored on a user's computer when you visit a website on the Internet. These files are designed to hold data specific to a particular client and website.

When you visit a website, it sends a cookie to your computer, where it is stored in a file. Only the website that creates a cookie can read it. Other servers cannot access this information.

These files typically contain information about your visit to the webpage or record your login information. This may not always be bad.

Chapter 4 Entrepreneurial Skills-II

The word 'entrepreneur' is derived from the French word 'entreprendre' which means "to do something" or "to undertake".

An entrepreneur is an individual who creates a new business, bearing most of the risks and enjoying most of the rewards.

The term **entrepreneurship** refers to the functions performed by an entrepreneur. It is the process involving various actions to be undertaken by the entrepreneur in establishing a new enterprise.

Entrepreneurship and Society

While the concept of entrepreneurship has a wide meaning, it describes as starting a business using the resources available to a person.

Entrepreneurship has some positive impact on society such as

- Accentuates economic growth
- Fosters creativity
- Stimulates innovation and efficiency
- Creates jobs and employment opportunities
- Solves the problems of the society
- Encourages welfare of the society

Society plays a role in boosting entrepreneurship by

- Creates needs and demands
- Provides raw materials
- Enables financial support
- Creates a need for education
- Catalyses policy formation and reform
- Facilitates networking
- Supports infrastructure development

Types of Entrepreneurship Activities

Some common entrepreneurship activities related to society include:

1. **Social Entrepreneurship** Social entrepreneurship can be understood as creation of sustainable solutions for social problems that leads to social change by employing entrepreneurial mindset, processes and operations. In social entrepreneurship, research is conducted to completely define a specific and core social problem.
2. **Agricultural Entrepreneurship** Agricultural Entrepreneurship can be defined as being primarily related to the marketing and production of inputs and products used in agricultural activities.
3. **Women Entrepreneurship** Women entrepreneurship is referred to the entrepreneurial activity led by women, where women undertake risks, create enterprises, organise factors of production, innovate with products/services and generate employment opportunities.
4. **Small Scale Entrepreneurship** Small scale entrepreneurship refers to starting industries in which manufacturing, trading, providing services, productions are done on a small scale or micro scale. These businesses serve as the backbone of many developing countries.

Characteristics/Qualities of Entrepreneur

For the successful enterprise, it is important to understand the characteristics/qualities of successful entrepreneurs and it is described below :

- **Leadership** An entrepreneur must possess the characteristics of leadership and must lead a team for achievement of goals. The leader is able to clearly articulate their ideas and has a clear vision.
- **Risk Taking** An entrepreneur with rational planning and firm decisions bear the risks. They have differentiated approach towards risks.
- **Innovativeness** With the changing needs and requirements of customers production should meet requirements with the help of innovative ideas.
- **Goal-oriented** Goal-oriented entrepreneurs achieve the maximum results from their efforts in business due to the fact they work towards clear and measurable targets.
- **Decision-Maker** An entrepreneur has to take many decisions to put his business idea into reality. He chooses the best suitable and profitable alternative.
- **Motivator** An entrepreneur has to create a spirit of team work and motivate them. So that he gets full cooperation from the employees.
- **Self-confident** An entrepreneur should have confidence to achieve his goals otherwise he won't be able to convince his team to achieve his goals.

- **Action-oriented** An entrepreneur should have an action oriented vision and ideology to plan things well.
- **Dynamic Agent** An entrepreneur creates new needs and new means to satisfy them. He has the ability to visualise new ventures and new plans.
- **High Achiever** Entrepreneurs are high achievers as they have a strong urge to achieve. The most important characteristic is his achievement motivation.
- **Trust in Self** An entrepreneur believes on their own decisions and actions as he has trust in his perseverance and creations. He does not believe in luck.

Functions of an Entrepreneur

The various functions of an entrepreneur are as follows

- **Innovation** It includes introducing new products, opening new markets, new sources of raw material and new organisation structure.
- **Risk-Taking** An entrepreneur has to take risk by choosing one among various alternatives.
- **Organisation and Management** An entrepreneur organise and manage various economic and human factors through planning, coordination, control, supervision and direction.
- **Size and Scale of Business Unit** An entrepreneur has to decide about the size of business unit as he wants to establish one production unit or more dependent upon the demand of the product.
- **Appointment of Managerial and Other Work Force** It is the entrepreneur who appoints the management staff as well as other work force as per the requirement and needs of the enterprise.
- **Factors of Production** The factors of production i.e. land, labour, capital etc., should be in appropriate proportion and to maximise output of these factors is the responsibility of the entrepreneur.
- **Control and Direction** He must exercise control over all departments and direct them on a timely basis.

Role and Significance of Entrepreneurs

The role and significance of entrepreneurs are as follows:

- **Organiser of Society's Productive Resources** An entrepreneur is the organiser of society's productive resources.
- **Helpful in Capital Formation** An entrepreneur is helpful in capital formation as we know that increase in the rate of capital formation is quite essential for the economic development of any country.
- **Increase in Employment Opportunities** An entrepreneur creates maximum employment opportunities in the society by way of establishing new industries, developing and expanding the existing industries and by undertaking innovative activities.
- **Development of New Production Techniques** An entrepreneur does not feel contended only with the existing techniques of production.
- **Visionary Leader** An entrepreneur has a good vision towards the achievement of his goals. He is able to recognise profitable opportunities and conceptualise strategies.
- **Higher Productivity** Entrepreneurs have the ability to produce more goods and services with less inputs. They play an important role in raising productivity.
- **Initiator** An entrepreneur is the one who initiates the process of creating an enterprise by coming up with the idea for the business and planning out how to turn that idea into reality.
- **Risk Taker** In an enterprise, an entrepreneur, being the owner, is the biggest risk taker.
- **Backbone of Capitalist System** Capitalist economy is one in which there is a freedom to save and invest to compete and operate any business.
- **Ingredient of Modern Production System** An entrepreneur has become the 'balancing wheel' of modern global economy. They seek the unique product, change the technical frontiers and reshape public desires.

Importance of Entrepreneurs

The importance of entrepreneurs are as follows

- **Free Market Evolution** In a free market, entrepreneurs are able to respond to changing customer preferences, prices, shifts in demand etc.
- **Efficiency Improvements** Entrepreneurs tend to adapt in an established business and increase their own efficiency.
- **New Markets** Entrepreneurs can often 'redefine the rules' of an established industry.

- **New Values** Sometimes, entrepreneurs choose ethics over profit and offer a more ethical product to the world and are transparent about it. For example, Jaipur rugs has multiple artisans who work towards making rugs that are sold around the world.

Myths about Entrepreneurship

Entrepreneurship is a set of activities performed by the entrepreneur. It is the process of identifying opportunities in the market place.

It is the attempt to create value. Many entrepreneurs believe a set of myths about entrepreneurship and the most common are as follows :

- **Starting a Business is Easy** In reality, it is a very difficult and challenging process to start a successful business. The rate of failure of new ventures is very high but small entrepreneurships are comparatively easier to start.
- **Lot of Money to Finance New Business** Successful entrepreneurs design their business with little cash also.
- **Start up's cannot be Financed** Under the schemes like MUDRA, entrepreneurs can raise loans from banks.
- **Talent is More Important than Industry** This is not true as the nature of industry an entrepreneur chooses greatly effects the success and growth of the business.
- **Most Start up's are Successful** Mostly in the developing countries start up's fail as they could not manage to earn high profits.

Entrepreneurship as a Career Option

Being an entrepreneur may appear as though an implausible profession to numerous youngsters. A few people are not even aware that having their very own business or independent work can be a choice.

Once the awareness of the two career choices comes in, it is important to understand how taking the route of entrepreneurship benefits an individual.

- Nurtures development of entrepreneurial skills and capabilities
- Enables application of an entrepreneurial mindset
- Develops the ability to handle failure and ambiguity
- Enhances critical thinking and problem-solving ability
- Provides early exposure to the real world
- Inspires to think about one's career differently
- Leads to creating difference in society

Chapter 5 Green Skills-II

Sustainable development is the development that satisfies the needs of the present without compromising the capacity of future generations, guaranteeing the balance between economic growth, care for the environment and social well-being.

The important principles of sustainable development are:

- To carefully utilise all resources.
- To conserve resources so that they meet the demands and requirements of the future generations.
- To minimise the depletion of natural resources.

The concept of sustainable development was popularised in 1987 by the United Nations World Commission on Environment and Development.

Importance of Sustainable Development

- Proper Use of Means and Resources
- Development of Positive Attitude
- Development Based on People's Participation
- Limitation of Development
- Long Lasting Development

Problems Related to Sustainable Development

- Poor management of natural resources
- Pollution exceeds
- Soil erosion, atmospheric pollution
- Effects of economic activities
- Observed to get worse as income rise.
- Rise in population is another problem
- Rise in demand for energy

Short-Term Solutions

- Illegal deforestation and smuggling of forest resources should be stopped.
- Proper balance ought to be maintained between deforestation and afforestation.
- Planning and building of industrial zones to manage and process are types of wastes.
- Proper treatment system, recycling of waste and their proper disposal should be undertaken.

- *Adoption of Rainwater Harvesting Techniques, drip/Sprinkler irrigation and use of alternative sources of energy.*
- *Polluting industries should be relocated outside the cities, far away from the populated areas.*

Long-Term Solutions

- *Government should make policies against illegal activities.*
- *Awareness campaigns*
- *Ecology must be protected*
- *Taxes and fines*
- *Sustainable agriculture must be promoted such as permaculture, agroforestry, mixed farming, multiple cropping and crop rotation.*

United Nations Sustainable Development Summit (2015) *sets global development goals. These goals are termed as Agenda 2030. The goals are:*

- *End poverty*
- *Hunger*
- *Healthy*
- *Quality education*
- *Gender equality*
- *Water and sanitation for all*
- *Affordable, reliable, sustainable and modern energy for all*
- *Sustainable economic growth*
- *Infrastructure, promote sustainable industrialisation and foster innovation*
- *Reduce inequality*
- *Make cities inclusive, safe, resilient and production.*
- *Sustainable consumption and production.*
- *Urgent action to combat climate change and its impacts.*
- *Conserve and sustainably use oceans, seas and marine resources.*
- *Sustainably manage forests, halt and reverse land degradation, halt biodiversity loss.*
- *Peaceful and inclusive societies.*
- *Global partnership for sustainable development.*

Part B (Subject Specific Skills)

Chapter 1 Digital Documentation (Advanced)

Word processing, spreadsheet and presentation are most common activities performed in an office. OfficeSuite software is used to perform these activities effectively.

A document is a paper with written contents and the process of preparing a document is called **documentation**.

Word processing software is used for the creation of text-based documents. It is a GUI based software used in the Windows environment. A word processor is a software package that processes textual matter and creates organised documents.

There are many software packages available to do the job of word processing. Some examples of word processing softwares are AppleWorks, Microsoft Word, StarOffice, TextMaker, WordPerfect, etc.

Features of Word Processor

Word processing packages have the following features

- Text editing
- Formatting text
- GUI Interface
- Mail merge
- Security of files
- Auto formatting
- OLE
- Graphics
- Language and grammar
- Online help option, etc.

LibreOffice Writer

LibreOffice Writer is an extension that allows to create, edit and view any documents. It is a free and open source word processor component of the LibreOffice software package you can use it to type letters, newsletters, reports and other documents. It provides tools for editing, formatting and printing of documents.

Advantages of Styles

Styles are used to make document more attractive and good. There are some advantages of styles as

- Styles are used to maintain the consistency of a document in different formatting.
- Style make major formatting changes easily replicable across all the objects that have the same style.

Categories/ Types of Styles in Writer

LibreOffice supports the following types of styles

Types of Styles	Description
Page Styles	This style affects the formatting and looks of page. It includes margins, headers and footers, borders and backgrounds.
Paragraph Styles	This style affects the full paragraph. When paragraph styles applied, it controls all aspects of a paragraph's appearance that include text alignment, tab stops, line spacing and borders. It can also include character formatting.
Character Styles	This style affects the block of characters of a paragraph. Character styles includes font, size, color or bold/italic formats.
Frame Styles	This style affects frames and graphics. Frame style is used to format text frames and graphic. It includes text wrap, borders, backgrounds and columns.
List Styles	This style allows you to select, format and position numbers or bullets in lists.

Style Groups

There are style groups that can display in the Styles and Formatting window

Style Groups	Description
Hierarchical	It displays the styles in hierarchical list.
All Styles	It displays all styles of selected style category.
Applied Styles	It displays the applied styles in document.
Custom Styles	It displays all user-defined styles.
Automatic	It displays styles that will be appropriate to the current context.
Text Styles	It displays styles that applied on text.
Chapter Styles	It displays formatting styles used for heading.
List Styles	It displays formatting styles used for number or bulleted list.

Index Styles	It displays formatting styles used for indexes.
Special Style	It displays formatting style used for headers, footnotes, tables etc.
HTML Style	It displays the styles used for HTML documents.
Conditional Styles	It displays styles used for user-defined condition.

Insert an Image from Gallery

The Gallery provides a convenient way to group reusable objects such as graphics and sounds that you can insert into your documents. The Gallery is available in all components of LibreOffice. It does not come with many graphics, but you can add your own pictures or find extensions containing more graphics.

Resizing a Drawing Object

Resizing a drawing object is done same as image resizing. To resize a drawing object, follow the below steps

Step 1. Click the object to show the green resizing handles.

Step 2. Position the pointer over one of the green resizing handles. The pointer changes shape giving a graphical representation of the direction of the resizing.

Step 3. Click and drag to resize the object.

Step 4. Release the mouse button when satisfied with the new size.

Grouping Drawing Objects

To group drawing objects, follow the below steps:

Step 1. Select an object, then hold down the Shift key and select the others you want to include in the group. The bounding box expands to include all the selected objects.

Step 2. With the objects selected, hover the mouse pointer over one of the objects and follow below steps :

- Choose Format tab.
- Select Group that will open sub menu.
- Select Group option.

To ungroup the objects, select Format→ Group → Ungroup.

Create and Use Template

A template is a model that you use to create other documents. For example, you can create a template for business reports that has your company's logo on the first page. New documents created from this template will all have your company's logo on the first page.

Create and Customise Table of Contents

Table of Content (TOC) is a list that used to show the contents of book or chapter with their respective page number. With the table of contents, you found number of chapters, name of chapters and page number of chapter where it began. Table of Content (TOC) is always given beginning of the book.

Hierarchy of Headings

Headings can be numbered or not; typically the first level headings in a book length document are chapter title, which may be numbered, but lower level headings are not numbered. Some heading styles number, each heading level for example 1, 1.1, 1.2, 2, 2.1 and so on. When chapters or sections are added or deleted, the numbering is automatically changed.

Implement Mail Merge

A mail merge is a way to take a letter you've written and send it to a whole bunch of people. A mail merge can also be a quick way to take a list of people's mailing addresses and generate labels or envelopes with the address for a different person on each label or envelope. It is essential for any person or organization that has a lot of clients, partners, or other people to communicate with.

To open a new document, follow the below steps

Step 1. Click on File tab

Step 2. Choose New and then select Text Document

Now, start the Mail Merge Wizard using Tools → Mail Merge Wizard. This will open the Mail Merge Wizard window.

Step 1. Select starting document

Step 2. Select document type

Step 3. Insert address block

- Selecting the data source (address list)
- Selecting the address block
- Matching the fields

Step 4. Create salutation

Step 5. Adjust layout

Step 6. Edit document and insert extra fields

Step 7. Personalise document

Step 8. Save, print or send

Chapter 2 Electronic Spreadsheet (Advanced)

An electronic spreadsheet is used for analysing, sharing and managing information for accounting purpose, performing mathematical calculations, budgeting, billing etc. A spreadsheet is a matrix of rows and columns similar to an accounting ledger. The spreadsheet program also provides tools for creating graphs and inserting pictures etc., for analysing the data etc. Some examples of spreadsheet software are Lotus 1-2-3, Quattro-Pro, MS-Excel, VisiCalc, LibreOffice Calc etc.

LibreOffice Calc

Calc is an easy to understand spreadsheet program that appeals to novice users and professional data miners and number crunchers alike.

Calc provides a number of features not present in Excel, including a system which automatically defines a series for graphing based on the layout of the users's data. Calc is also capable of writing spreadsheets directly as PDF files.

Consolidating data

Data Consolidation allows you to gather together your data from separate worksheets into a master worksheet. In other words, the Data Consolidation function takes data from a series of worksheets or workbooks and summaries it into a single worksheet that you can update easily.

SUBTOTAL is a function listed under the Mathematical category when you use the Function Wizard

(Insert → Function). Because of its usefulness, the function has a graphical interface. It is accessible from Data menu.

What -if Analysis

What-if analysis is the study of how the uncertainty in the output of a model or system can be linked to different sources of uncertainty in its inputs. Its main purpose is to test the robustness of the results of a model or system in the presence of uncertainty to better understand the relationship between input and output variables in a system or model.

What-if analysis searches for errors in the model through unexpected relationship between inputs and outputs.

LibreOffice Calc provides these tools for What-if Analysis:

Using Scenarios

Scenarios are a tool to test "what-if" questions. Each scenario is named, and can be edited and formatted separately. When you print the spreadsheet, only the content of the currently active scenario is printed.

Using Goal Seek

Goal seeking is the process of finding the correct input value when only the output is known. The function of goal seeking can be built into different kinds of computer software programs like LibreOffice Calc.

Using the Solver

Solver is a more descriptive form of Goal Seek. Solver can deal with multiple variables as the Goal Seek is used to manipulate one variable cell. It is specifically designed to minimize or maximize the result according to a set of rules that you define.

Working with Hyperlinks

Hyperlinks can be used in Calc to jump to a different location from within a spreadsheet and can lead to other parts of the current file, to different files or even to web sites.

Types of Hyperlink

There are two types of hyperlinks in Calc as

- *Absolute link*
- *Relative link*

*An **absolute link** will stop working only if the target is moved. A **relative link** will stop working only if the start and target locations change relative to each other.*

Macros

A macro is a saved sequence of commands or keystrokes that are stored for later use. The LibreOffice.org (OOo) macro language is very flexible, allowing automation of both simple and complex tasks. Macros are especially useful to repeat a task the same way over and over again.

Sorting

Sorting data can be automated in Open Office by creating a Macro in Calc. Data can be sorted on a single column or more than one column. Each time the Macro runs the data gets sorted. Such macros can be written using code in Open Office.

Chapter 3 Database Management System

Database Concept

A database is a collection of logically related information/data, which is available for one or more users organised in a way, so that it can be easily accessed, managed and updated. It is actually a place, where related piece of information is stored and various operations can be performed on it by the user.

Components of a Database

A database consists of several components. Each component plays an important role in the database system environment.

The major components of database are as follows:

Data

It is raw numbers, characters or facts represented by value. Most of the organisations generate, store and process large amount of data.

Software

It is a set of programs that lies between the stored data and the users of database. It is used to control and manage the overall computerised database.

Hardware

It is the physical aspect of computer, telecommunication and database, which consists of the secondary storage devices such as magnetic disks, optical discs etc., on which data is stored.

Users

It is the person, who needs information from the database to carry out its primary business responsibilities. The various types of users which can access the database system are as follows:

- Database administrator (DBA)
- Application programmer
- End-user

Features of a Database

Features of a database to let you manage your data are as follows:

Tables

It is the building block of any relational database model, where all the actual data is defined and entered. A database consists of many tables. Tables (relations) consist of cells at the intersection of records (rows) and fields (columns).

- **Fields or Columns (Data item)** It is an area (within the record), reserved for a specific piece of data. It is the individual sub-component of one record. It contains set of characters.
- **Records or Rows or Tuples** It is the collection of data items of all the fields (information) pertaining to one entity or a complete unit of information, i.e. a person, company, transition etc.

Queries

It is an inquiry into the database using the SELECT statement. These statements give you filtered data according to your conditions and specifications indicating the fields, records and summaries which a user wants to fetch from a database.

Forms

In a database, a form is a window or a screen that contains numerous fields or spaces to enter data. Forms can be used to view and edit your data. It is an interface in user specified layout.

Reports

When you want to print those records which are fetched from your database, design a report. It is an effective way to present data in a printed format.

Database Server

The term database server may refer to both hardware and software used to run a database, according to the context.

Database Management System (DBMS)

It is a collection of programs that enables users to create, maintain database and control all the access to the database. It is a computer based record keeping system. Some basic processes that are supported by a DBMS are as follows:

- Specification of data types, structures and constraints to be considered in an application.
- Storing the data itself into persistent storage.
- Manipulation of the database.
- Querying the database to retrieve desired information.
- Updating the content of the database.

Data Integrity

Data Integrity ensures the accuracy, reliability and consistency of the data during any operation.

Each type of data integrity are as follows:

- **Entity Integrity** *It defines the primary key of a table. Entity integrity rule on a column does not allow duplicate and null values.*
- **Domain Integrity** *It defines the type, range and format of data allowed in a column. Domain integrity states that all values in a column must be of same type.*
- **Referential Integrity** *It defines the foreign key concepts. Referential integrity ensures that data in related tables remains accurate and consistent before and after changes.*
- **User Defined Integrity** *If there is some business requirements which do not fit any above data integrity then user can create own integrity, which is called user defined integrity.*

Key Fields

The key is defined as the column or the set of columns of the database table which is used to identify each record uniquely in a relation. If a table has id, name and address as the column names then each one is known as the key for that table. The key field is a unique identifier for each record.

The following are the types of key fields available in the DBMS system:

Primary Key

A field or a set of fields that uniquely identify each record in a table is known as a primary key. Each relation has atleast one column for which each row that must have a unique value. Only one column attribute can be defined as a primary key for each table.

Candidate Key

The set of all attributes which can uniquely identify each tuple of a relation are known as candidate keys. Each table may have one or more candidate keys and one of them will become the primary key. The candidate key of a relation is always a minimal key.

Alternate Key

From the set of candidate keys after selecting one of the keys as a primary key, all other remaining keys are known as alternate keys.

Foreign Key

A field of a table (relation) that references the primary key of another table is referred to as foreign key. The relationship between two tables is established with the help of foreign key.

RDBMS (Relational Database Management System)

A relational database is a type of database. It uses a structure that allows us to identify and access data in relation to another piece of data in the database. Often, data in a relational database is organized into tables.

Data Types

Data types are used to identify which type of data (value), we are going to store in the database.

Fields themselves can be of different types depending on the data they contain. Data types in LibreOffice base are broadly classified into five categories listed below

- *Numeric types*
- *Alphanumeric types*
- *Binary types*
- *Date time*
- *Other variable types*

Manipulating Data

In a database, structure and manipulation of data are done by some commands. For this, we can use SQL commands. SQL (Structured Query Language) commands are the instructions used to communicate with the database to perform specific task that work with data.

Data Definition Language (DDL)

DDL is used to define the structure of your tables and other objects in the database. In DBMS, it is used to specify a database schema as a set of definitions (expressed in DDL). In SQL, the Data Definition Language allows you to create, alter and destroy database objects.

Data definition language consists of various commands that lets you to perform some specified tasks as follows

- **CREATE** *Uses to create objects in the database.*
- **ALTER** *Uses to alter the structure of the database table. This command can add up additional columns,*

drop existing columns and even change the data type of columns involved in a database table.

- **DROP** Uses to delete objects from the database.
- **TRUNCATE** Uses to remove all records from a table.
- **RENAME** Uses to rename an object.

Data Manipulation Language (DML)

DML provides various commands used to access and manipulate data in existing database. This manipulation involves inserting data into database tables, retrieving existing data, deleting data from existing tables and modifying existing data.

Various data manipulation language commands are as follows

- **SELECT** Used to retrieve data from a database.
- **INSERT** Used to insert data into a table.
- **UPDATE** Used to update existing data within a table.
- **DELETE** Used to delete all records from a table, the space of the records remains.

Transaction Control Language (TCL)

TCL commands are used to manage transactions in database. These are also used to manage the changes made by DML statements. It allows statements to be grouped together into logical transactions. A transaction is a single unit of work.

Various transaction control commands are as follows

- **COMMIT** Used to save the work done.
- **SAVEPOINT** Used to identify a point in a transaction to which you can later rollback.
- **ROLLBACK** Used to restore database to original, since the last COMMIT.
- **SET TRANSACTION** It establishes properties for the current transactions.

Data Control Language (DCL)

DCL commands are used to assign security levels in database which involves multiple user setups. They are used to grant defined role and access privileges to the users. Two types of DCL commands run on

- **GRANT** Used to give user's access privileges to database.
- **REVOKE** Used to withdraw access privileges given with the GRANT command.

Introduction to Form

Forms are used for entering, modifying and viewing records you likely have had to fill out forms on many occasions, like when visiting a doctor's clinic, applying for a job or registering for school.

When you enter information in a form in Base, the data goes exactly where the database designer wants it to go: in one or more related tables.

Chapter 4 Maintain Health, Safety and Secure Working Environment

Maintain Workplace Safety

Every organisation must follow a standard set of safety rules and procedures. These rules must be stated and displayed clearly at important areas.

Basic safety rules to follow at workplace are Fire safety, Falls and slips, Electrical safety, Use of first aid etc.

Basic Fire Safety Rules

Most of the time fire can be prevented using appropriate measures.

- Fire escape plans must be installed at proper levels
- Conduct regular drills.
- Smoke alarms must be placed at proper intervals.
- Keep workplace a no-smoking zone.
- Maintenance of safety equipment must be taken care of regularly.

Falls and Slips Safety Rules

- Keep the moving area clean and clutter free.
- Workplace must be proper ventilated receive light.
- Wear non-slippery footwear.
- Floors must be clean and dry.
- Oil spills, dust must be immediately cleaned.

Electrical Safety Rules:

- Electrical equipment used should be approved by a recognised organisation.
- Workers should be trained to handle the electric equipment safely.
- Damaged and hazardous electrical equipment should be immediately replaced. All old and workout and frayed switches and wires should be changed.

- *Heat emanating equipment should be kept away from the electrical equipment.*
- *Take care that the outlets/ circuits should not be overloaded .*
- *Switch off and unplug the electrical appliances before cleaning or relocating them.*

Use of First Aid

First Aid is the immediate assistance provided to the injured to save life and minimize health loss till the proper medical aid/ facility is provided.

Some rules of First Aid are :

- *Assure the injured to remain calm and not to panic.*
- *Keep them warm if they are under shock.*
- *Do not move the victim in case of back/neck injury.*

Occupational Hazards of Workplace

A worker may face Occupational hazards at workplace. : An occupational hazard is the illness one may acquire due to his occupation.

Like people working in a chemical factory may get affected due to presence of certain chemicals. Some types of occupational hazards are : Physical hazards, chemical hazards, biological hazards, , behavioural hazards, radiological hazards, ergonomic hazards etc.

Case studies of hazardous situation

Following are the examples of hazardous situation when the safety steps are missing or are not followed properly.

CASE Study 1 : Hazards due to Chemicals

From past 3 years Rahul worked in a chemical factory where some types of Acids are being manufactured. He is supposed to carry a sample of chemical in a special flask with a tight cap.

He went to take the sample from the dispenser and did not fixed the cap properly. While carrying the chemical back he slipped and because the cap was not fixed and the chemical spilled over, lower half of his face and one hand. The worker suffered from severe burns due to chemical burns.

CASE Study 2 : Hazards due to Electric shocks

A 30 year old servant was electrocuted and lost control over his limbs while doing some house chores. After investigating, it was found that insulation of the electric wire from the night lamp was cracked and full 220 volt current was live on the lamp pole.

This meant the wire was not inspected regularly. Otherwise, the damaged insulated wire should have been changed and replaced with a new safe to touch wire

CASE Study 3: Hazards due to Fire

A storekeeper was in a habit of throwing the plastic waste and packing waste in the backdoor of his store. The housekeeping staff was in a habit of smoking cigarette during their break time.

One week the pile of plastic and packing garbage was not cleaned. One of the housekeeping staff just threw the discarded cigarette in that garbage heap of plastics and packing material.

As the day was hot and sunny, the garbage caught fire. By the time the fire was noticed, fire flames engulfed the whole back area causing heavy damage to the store and the backdoor area.

The fire could have been prevented if the storekeeper had taken appropriate garbage disposal measures, restricting smoking in the premises.

Prevent Accidents and Emergencies

Accident: is an unplanned event that may happen all of a sudden and may lead to unwanted or unprecedented results/outcomes.

Types of Accidents

Accidents may be of following types :

- *Accidents at workplace : Slips and fall accidents, fire*
- *Industrial disease/illness*
- *Road traffic accidents*
- *Clinical Accidents*
- *Sports related accidents*

Handling Accidents:

Accidents must be handled carefully. The accident should be handled compassionately without assigning blame on others.

- *Every organisation must follow SOP (Standard Operating Procedure) for accident handling.*
- *Safety measures must be placed to prevent workplace accidents.*
- *Immediately call the medical team for any injury.*
- *Stay alert.*
- *Pay attention to and follow emergency drills.*